180 Days Printing
Advanced

MW00851755

Publishing Credits

Corinne Burton, M.A.Ed., *Publisher*
Emily R. Smith, M.A.Ed., *Senior VP of Content Development*
Véronique Bos, *Vice President of Creative*
Andrew Greene, M.A.Ed., *Senior Content Manager*
Jill Malcolm, *Graphic Designer*

Standards

© Copyright 2007–2021 Texas Education Agency (TEA). All Rights Reserved.
© 2012 English–Language Arts Content Standards for California Public Schools by the California Department of Education.
© Copyright 2010 National Governors Association Center for Best Practices and Council of Chief State School Officers. All rights reserved.

Image Credits: all images from iStock and/or Shutterstock

The classroom teacher may reproduce copies of materials in this book for classroom use only. The reproduction of any part for an entire school or school system is strictly prohibited. No part of this publication may be transmitted, stored, or recorded in any form without written permission from the publisher.

Website addresses included in this book are public domain and may be subject to changes or alterations of content after publication of this product. Shell Education does not take responsibility for the future accuracy or relevance and appropriateness of website addresses included in this book. Please contact the company if you come across any inappropriate or inaccurate website addresses, and they will be corrected in product reprints.

All companies, websites, and products mentioned in this book are registered trademarks of their respective owners or developers and are used in this book strictly for editorial purposes. No commercial claim to their use is made by the author or the publisher.

A division of Teacher Created Materials
5482 Argosy Avenue
Huntington Beach, CA 92649
www.tcmpub.com/shell-education
ISBN 978-1-0876-6242-8
© 2023 Shell Educational Publishing, Inc.
Printed in USA. WOR004

Table of Contents

Introduction

Foundations for Handwriting 5

Getting Ready to Write 6

Letter Presentation Order 8

Sight Words 9

How to Use This Book 10

Weekly Practice Pages

Week 1: *Ll* 13

Week 2: *Tt* 18

Week 3: *Ii* 23

Week 4: 1 28

Week 5: *Ff* 33

Week 6: *Ee* 38

Week 7: *Dd* 43

Week 8: 2 48

Week 9: *Pp* 53

Week 10: *Bb* 58

Week 11: *Rr* 63

Week 12: 3 68

Week 13: *Nn* 73

Week 14: *Mm* 78

Week 15: *Aa* 83

Week 16: 4 88

Week 17: *Hh* 93

Week 18: *Kk* 98

Week 19: 5 103

Week 20: *Uu* 108

Week 21: *Vv* 113

Week 22: 6 118

Week 23: *Ww* 123

Table of Contents *(cont.)*

Weekly Practice Pages

Week 24: *Xx* 128

Week 25: 7 133

Week 26: *Yy* 138

Week 27: *Zz* 143

Week 28: 8 148

Week 29: *Cc* 153

Week 30: *Oo* 158

Week 31: 9 163

Week 32: *Qq* 168

Week 33: *Gg* 173

Week 34: 0 178

Week 35: *Ss* 183

Week 36: *Jj* 188

Appendix

Lowercase Letter Guide 193

Uppercase Letter Guide. 196

Number Guide 199

Suggested Websites 200

Digital Resources 200

© Shell Education

Foundations for Handwriting

Welcome to *180 Days of Printing: Advanced*! Students will learn the foundations for handwriting and practice letter formation basics in this book. These practice pages provide fun and engaging ways for young learners to develop good handwriting habits.

Hand-eye Coordination

Hand-eye coordination is essential for handwriting. Students track lines with their eyes to guide, direct, and control hand movement. Coordination allows students to write on the line, properly space letters, write proper letter size, and more. This developmental approach is also seen in research-based programs such as Handwriting Without Tears. Hand-eye coordination is reinforced throughout this book through engaging, age-appropriate activities and practice pages.

Shapes

Drawing shapes provides a foundation for letter formation. As students become more familiar with using strokes to write basic shapes, they become more capable of writing letters. Shapes help bridge the gap between the general strokes of drawing and the strokes that will later form letters.

Drawing

Drawing helps students develop fine-motor skills that extend to handwriting, such as holding a writing instrument correctly and applying the correct amount of force and speed to mark paper. Drawing also helps students with basic line formation. Drawing keeps young writers engaged through play-based activities and practice pages.

Coloring

Coloring reinforces basic stroke formation along with hand-eye coordination. Coloring helps students develop fine-motor skills used in letter formation. Students also practice spacing, which is essential for writing words and sentences.

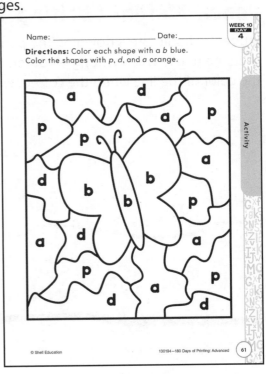

Getting Ready to Write

Pencil Grip

Students will naturally find their dominant hand as they learn to properly grip writing instruments. Help students decide which hand is more comfortable to write with, and guide them to alternate hands if they show no clear preference. Teach students a pencil grip with their pointer finger on the top, thumb on the side, and three fingers below the pencil to support the grip. Encourage students to use this pencil grip as they work through the pages of the book.

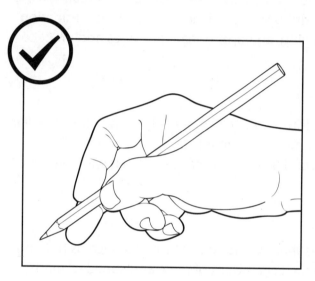 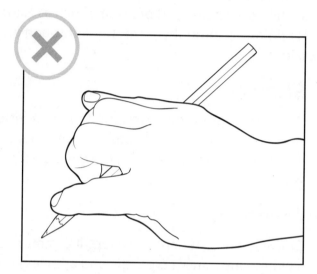

Pencil Weight (Writing Too Hard or Too Soft)

Students should press down on the pencil with medium weight. Demonstrate the proper pressure to use when writing—not too hard and not too soft. Bring students' attention to the color of the line when the correct weight is used.

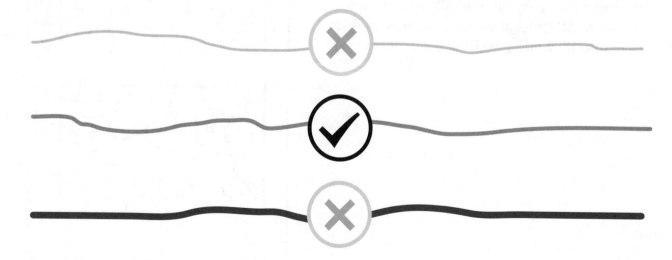

© Shell Education

Letter Spacing

Teach students proper letter spacing within a word and between words in a sentence. Demonstrate that letters in a word do not touch but have minimal space between them. As students grasp spacing within words, demonstrate the required spacing between words. Encourage students to use their pointer fingers or popsicle sticks to properly space the words. Reinforce letter spacing as students practice writing uppercase and lowercase letters on the review pages.

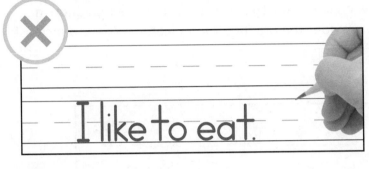

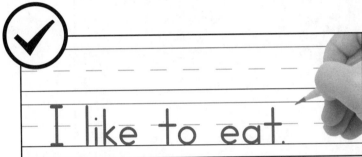

Letter Reversal

Some letter reversal is natural as students learn to write, especially with *p, q, d,* and *b.* Be sure to correct students in the case that they reverse letters and encourage quality letter formation instead of quantity. Provide adequate practice time so students understand the strokes for each particular letter. Letters in this program are presented by strokes to encourage a focus on letter directionality and order.

Letter Presentation Order

To give students a strong foundation in handwriting, this book builds off the smallest handwriting units—strokes. By presenting letters by strokes instead of alphabetical order, students can more easily make connections on how to write them. The letter presentation order also takes high-frequency letters into account, quickly providing a foundation to begin writing words and sentences. Presenting letters by stroke also gives students ample practice time to create and refine motor control when creating letter strokes. The use of repetition in presenting strokes across multiple weeks provides the practice young learners need to increase proficiency.

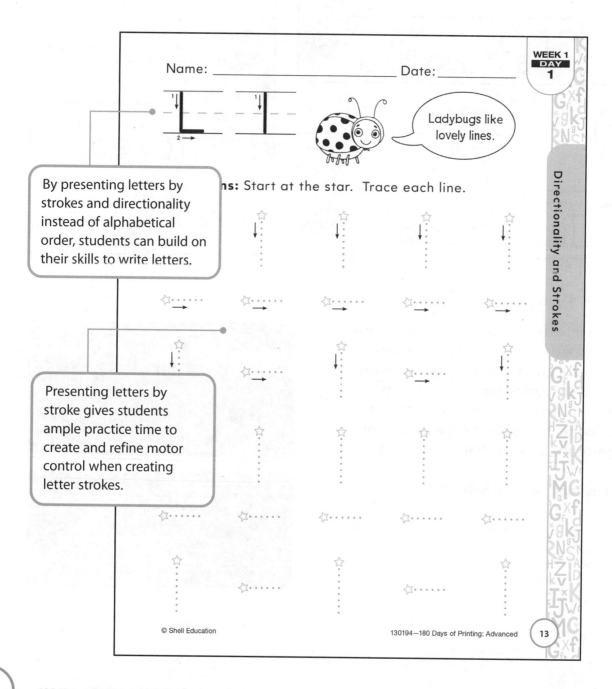

By presenting letters by strokes and directionality instead of alphabetical order, students can build on their skills to write letters.

Presenting letters by stroke gives students ample practice time to create and refine motor control when creating letter strokes.

© Shell Education

Sight Words

This program takes a holistic approach to handwriting, teaching not only individual letters but also how they fit into words and sentences. High-frequency words pulled from Dr. Edward Fry's Instant Words list and Dr. Edward Dolch's Most Common Words list allow students to practice words they will see and write frequently. The use of these sight words to practice handwriting increases letter awareness as students are exposed to these letters and words in other age-appropriate learning materials.

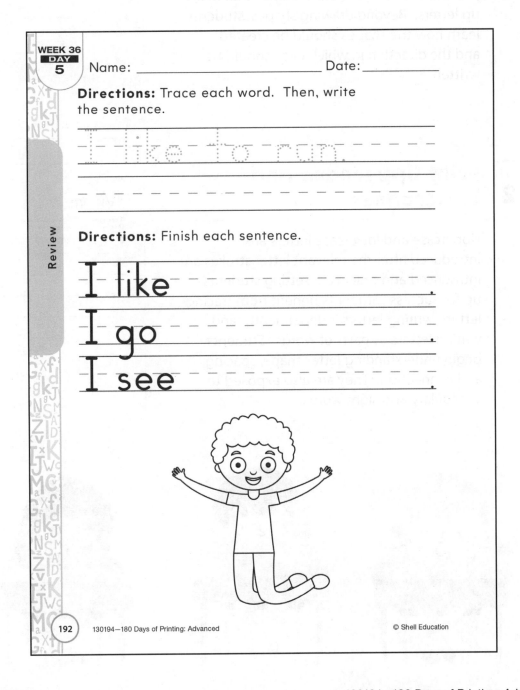

How to Use This Book

Day 1

Directionality and Strokes

180 Days of Printing: Advanced prioritizes giving students a strong foundation as they begin writing. Before each letter is introduced, students have a chance to practice strokes—the basic shapes that make up letters. Beyond drawing shapes, students learn how the shapes should be created and the direction in which each should be written.

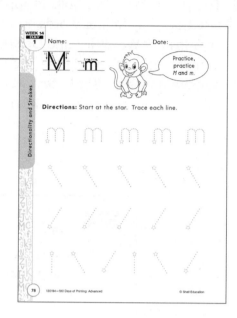

Day 2

Print Uppercase and Lowercase

Uppercase and lowercase letters are introduced after the relevant letter strokes are introduced and practiced, setting students up for success. Students benefit from tracing letters, writing letters independently, and writing letters as parts of words. Students begin understanding letter shape, spacing, and connection. They are also exposed to vocabulary and sight words.

© Shell Education

Day 3 — Sentence Practice

Students practice words and sentences with the sample letter. By practicing using the letters in sentences, students demonstrate spatial awareness and practice proper punctuation. Students practice the letter presented through alliterative sentences and writing prompts. Students are provided multiple opportunities to continue writing letters introduced in previous activities as well.

Day 4 — Activity

Activities give students chances to practice strokes, directionality, and letter recognition in engaging ways. These activities focus on developing fine-motor skills while building on letter recognition.

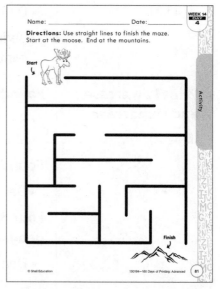

Day 5 — Review

A key to mastering handwriting is repetition. Weekly reviews provide students with extra practice. The reviews build on previous skills to practice letter spacing and connections and move toward more independent writing. The reviews also provide opportunities to practice sight words through repetition.

Standards Correlations

Shell Education is committed to producing educational materials that are research and standards based. To support this effort, this resource is correlated to the academic standards of all 50 states, the District of Columbia, the Department of Defense Dependent Schools, and the Canadian provinces. A correlation is also provided for key professional educational organizations.

To print a customized correlation report for your state, please visit our website at **www.tcmpub.com/administrators/correlations** and follow the online directions. If you require assistance in printing correlation reports, please contact the Customer Service Department at 1-800-858-7339.

Stroke and Directionality (Day 1)	**Foundational Skills: Adjust grasp and body position for increased control in drawing and writing.** • Demonstrate proper finger grasp. • Begin using nondominant hand to hold paper to maintain control.
Print Lowercase and Uppercase (Day 2)	**Foundational Skills: Print all upper- and lowercase letters.** • Recognize and print all upper- and lowercase letters of the alphabet. **Foundational Skills: Capitalize dates and names of people.** • Demonstrate understanding of capitalization. **Foundational Skills: Capitalize holidays, product names, and geographic names.** • Demonstrate understanding of capitalization.
Sentence Practice (Day 3)	**Foundational Skills: Use end punctuation for sentences.** • Demonstrate understanding of the organization and basic features of print.
Activity (Day 4)	**Foundational Skills: Practice words phonetically, drawing on phonemic awareness and spelling conventions.** • Demonstrate the ability to decode new vocabulary through phonemic and spelling awareness.
Review (Day 5)	**Foundational Skills: Use frequently occurring nouns and verbs.** • Begin reading and writing high-frequency nouns and verbs. • Demonstrate basic comprehension of nouns and verbs through sight words.

Name: _____ Date: _____

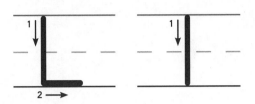

Ladybugs like lovely lines.

Directions: Start at each star. Connect the dots.

Name: _____   Date: _____

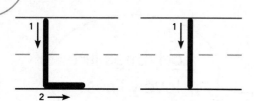

Directions: Follow the arrows. Trace each letter.
Then, write your own letters to fill the lines.

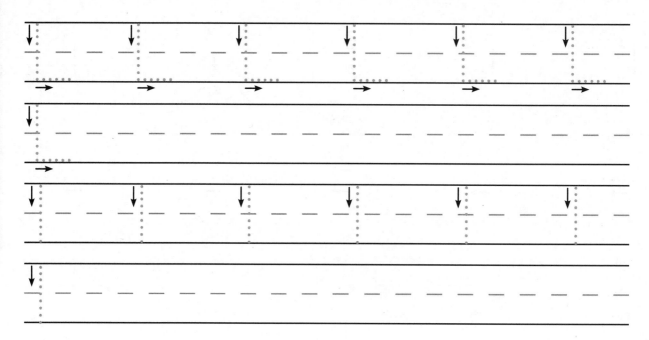

Print Uppercase and Lowercase

© Shell Education

Name: _____ Date: _____

Directions: Trace the letters. Then, write the missing letter to complete each word.

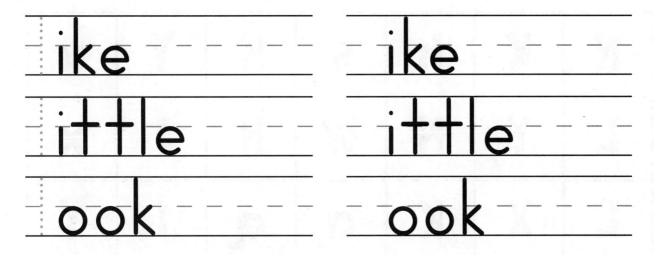

ike   ike

ittle   ittle

ook   ook

Directions: Trace the letters. Then, write the missing letters to complete the sentence.

uke ikes ions.

uke ikes ions.

© Shell Education

Sentence Practice

Name: _____ Date: _____

Directions: Color the squares with *L* green and *l* blue.
Then, color the remaining letters yellow.

Activity

N	K	h	s	K	Y	u
L	Y	N	W	H	I	x
L	X	K	a	q	l	Y
L	J	d	j	E	I	D
L	S	H	k	p	l	G
L	R	B	Y	X	I	Z
L	M	K	H	v	l	e
L	L	L	L	Y	I	N
O	Y	H	c	P	E	K

    © Shell Education

Name: _____ Date: _____

Directions: Trace each letter. Then, write your own letters to fill the lines.

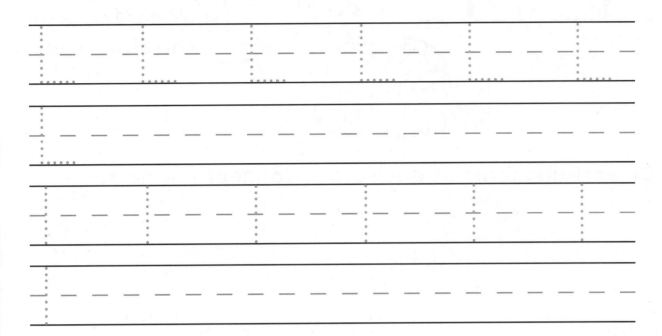

Directions: Trace the letters. Then, write the missing letter to complete each word or name.

ittle   ittle

ive   ive

ucy   ucy

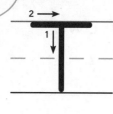

Name: _____ Date: _____

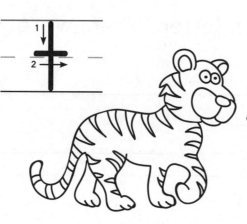

Directionality and Strokes

Getting these lines straight will make your letters look great!

Directions: Start at each star. Connect the dots.

© Shell Education

Name: _____ Date: _____

Directions: Follow the arrows. Trace each letter. Then, write your own letters to fill the lines.

Name: _____ Date: _____

Directions: Trace the letters. Then, write the missing letter to complete each word.

Sentence Practice

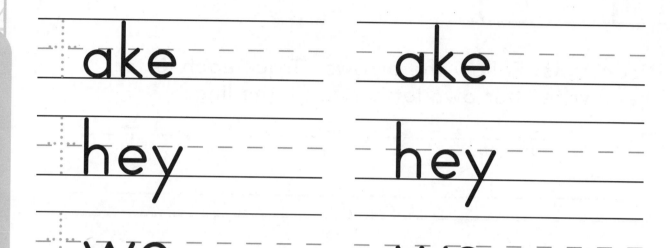

ake   ake

hey   hey

wo   wo

Directions: Trace the letters. Then, write the missing letters to complete the sentence.

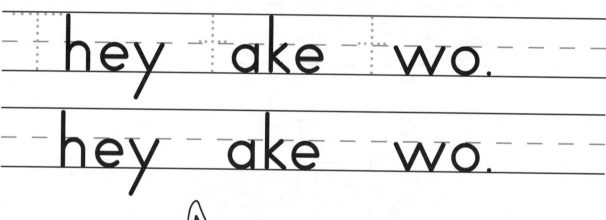

hey ake wo.

hey ake wo.

 130194—180 Days of Printing: Advanced © Shell Education

Name: _____ Date: _____

Directions: Use straight lines to complete the maze.

Activity

Start

Finish

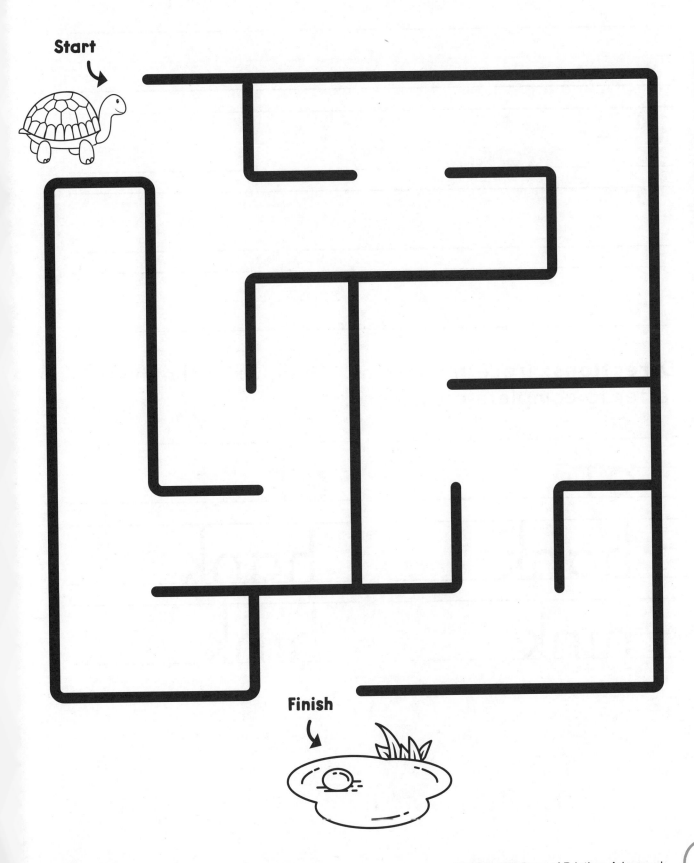

© Shell Education

Name: _____ Date: _____

Review

Directions: Trace each letter. Then, write your own letters to fill the lines.

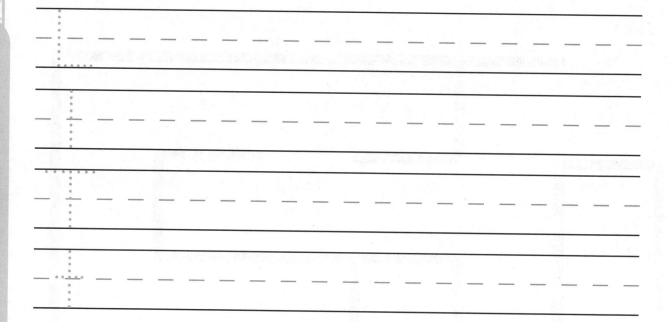

Directions: Trace the letters. Then, write the missing letter to complete each word.

© Shell Education

Name: _____ Date: _____

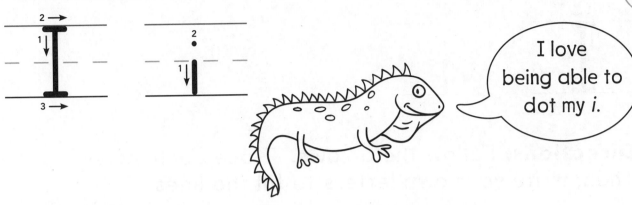

Directionality and Strokes

Directions: Place a dot in each circle.

Directions: Start at each star. Connect the dots.

© Shell Education   130194—180 Days of Printing: Advanced   23

Name: _____ Date: _____

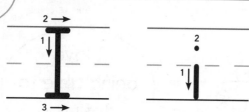

Directions: Follow the arrows. Trace each letter. Then, write your own letters to fill the lines.

130194—180 Days of Printing: Advanced

© Shell Education

Print Uppercase and Lowercase

Name: _____ Date: _____

Directions: Trace the letters. Then, write the missing letter to complete each word.

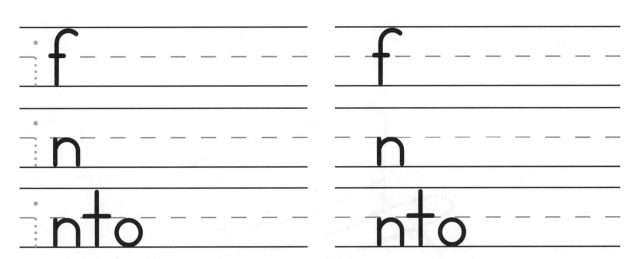

f

f

n

n

nto

nto

Directions: Trace the letters. Then, write the missing letters to complete the sentence.

I sa l kes ce cream.

I sa l kes ce cream.

© Shell Education

Sentence Practice

Name: _____ Date: _____

Directions: Put a dot in each circle. Then, color the picture.

130194—180 Days of Printing: Advanced   © Shell Education

Name: _____ Date: _____

Directions: Trace each letter. Then, write your own letters to fill the lines.

Review

Directions: Trace the letters. Then, write the missing letter to complete each word or name.

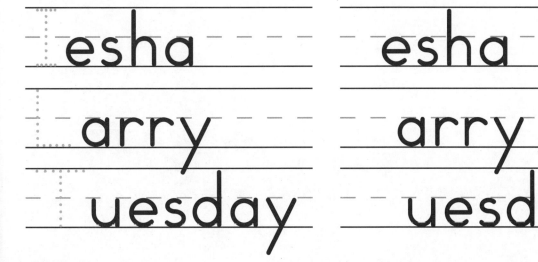

esha   esha

arry   arry

uesday   uesday

Name: _____ Date: _____

Directionality and Strokes

1 ↓
2 →

Top to bottom,
left to right, that's
the way we write,
write, write!

Directions: Start at each star. Connect the dots.

© Shell Education

Name: _____   Date: _____

1 one

Directions: Trace each number. Then, complete each number.

0	0	5	5
1	1	6	6
2	2	7	7
3	3	8	8
4	4	9	9

Name: _____ Date: _____

Directions: Trace the numbers to complete each math problem.

$$1 + 1 = 2$$

$$10 + 1 = 11$$

$$11 - 1 = 10$$

Directions: Solve each math problem.

$$1 + 10 = \underline{\hspace{2cm}}$$

$$12 + 1 = \underline{\hspace{2cm}}$$

130194—180 Days of Printing: Advanced

© Shell Education

Name: _____ Date: _____

Directions: Trace each line. Then, color the picture.

Name: _____ Date: _____

Directions: Trace each letter and number. Then, write your own letters and numbers to fill the lines.

Review

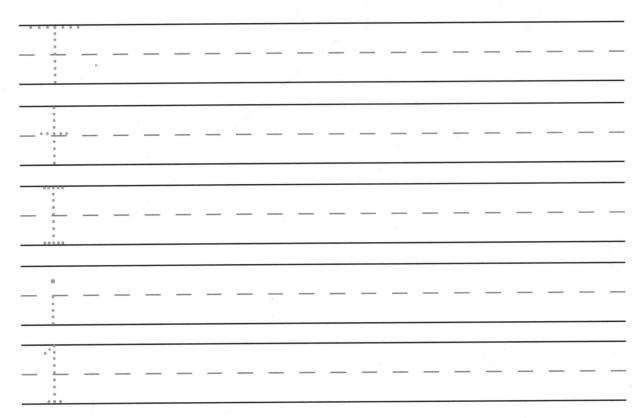

Directions: Trace the letters. Then, write the missing letters to complete the words.

© Shell Education

Name: _____ Date: _____

Straight lines
and curved lines
make an *f*.

Directions: Start at each star. Connect the dots.

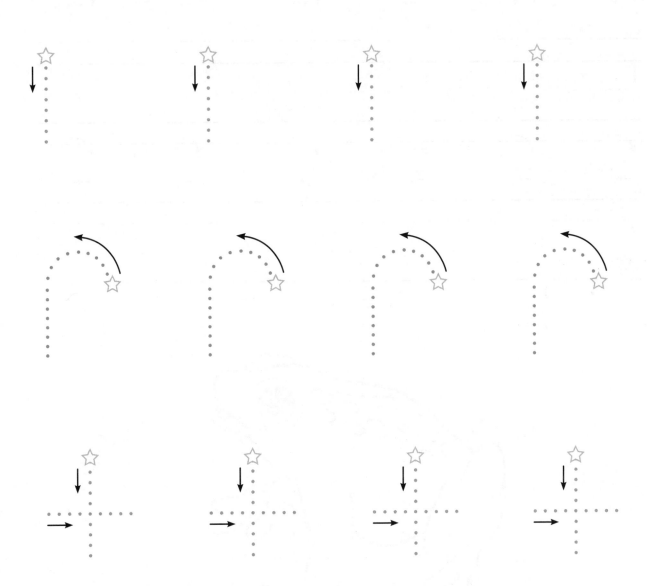

Name: _____ Date: _____

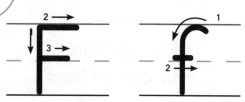

Directions: Follow the arrows. Trace each letter. Then, write your own letters to fill the lines.

Print Uppercase and Lowercase

© Shell Education

Name: _____ Date: _____

Directions: Trace the letters. Then, write the missing letter to complete each word.

find   find

first   first

from   from

Directions: Trace the letters. Then, write the missing letters to complete the sentence.

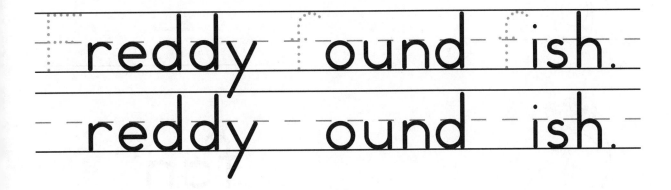

Freddy found fish.

Freddy found fish.

Sentence Practice

Name: _____ Date: _____

Directions: Match each word to a picture. Then, write the words.

Activity

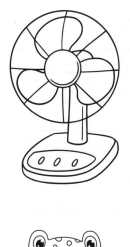

frog

frog

fish

fan

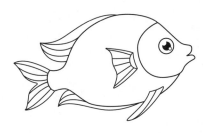

fox

    © Shell Education

Name: _____ Date: _____

Directions: Trace each letter. Then, write your own letters to fill the lines.

Directions: Trace the letters. Then, write the missing letters to complete the words.

y
or
ve

y
or
ve

Name: _____ Date: _____

Short straight line and round like c, that's the way to make an e.

Directionality and Strokes

Directions: Start at each star. Connect the dots.

Name: _____ Date: _____

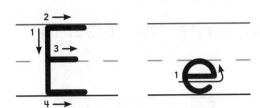

Directions: Follow the arrows. Trace each letter.
Then, write your own letters to fill the lines.

© Shell Education

Print Uppercase and Lowercase

Name: _____ Date: _____

Directions: Trace the letters. Then, write the missing letters to complete the words.

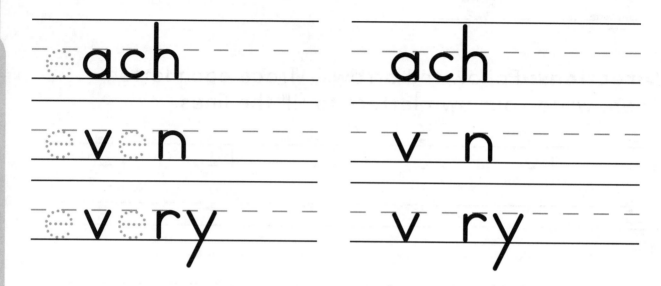

each   ach

even   v n

every   v ry

Directions: Trace the letters. Then, write the missing letters to complete the sentence.

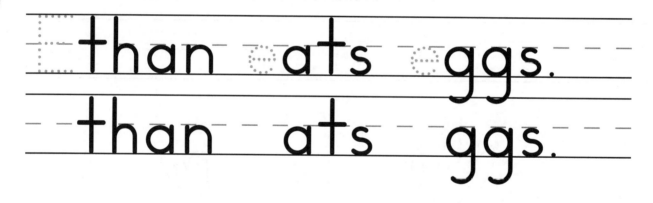

Ethan eats eggs.

than ats ggs.

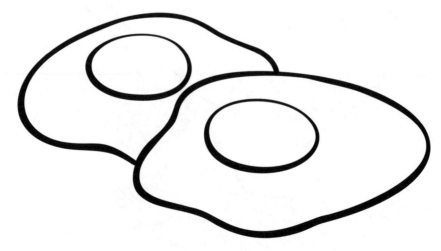

© Shell Education

Sentence Practice

Name: _____ Date: _____

Directions: Use the key. Match the letters to the numbers to write the words.

a	b	c	d	e	f	g	h	i	j	k	l	m
1	2	3	4	5	6	7	8	9	10	11	12	13

n	o	p	q	r	s	t	u	v	w	x	y	z
14	15	16	17	18	19	20	21	22	23	24	25	26

___ ___
9   20

___ ___ ___
12   5   20

___ ___ ___ ___
12   9   6   5

___ ___ ___ ___
12   5   6   20

© Shell Education

Name: _____ Date: _____

Directions: Trace each letter. Then, write your own letters to fill the lines.

Directions: Trace the letters. Then, write the missing letter to complete each word.

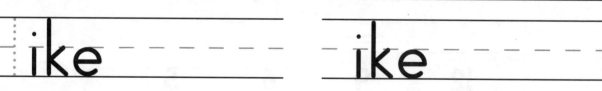

Review

Name: _____ Date: _____

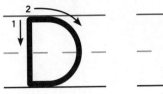 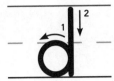 

A circle and line make a *d*.

Directions: Trace each circle. Then, practice writing O.

Directions: Write an O on each line.

Directionality and Strokes

WEEK 7 DAY 1

Name: _____   Date: _____

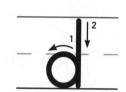

Directions: Follow the arrows. Trace each letter. Then, write your own letters to fill the lines.

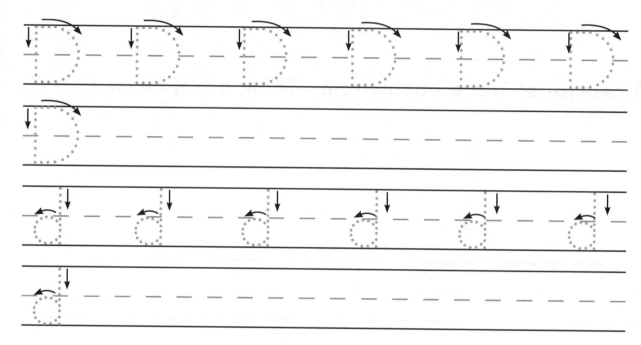

Print Uppercase and Lowercase

© Shell Education

Name: _____ Date: _____

Directions: Trace the letters. Then, write the missing letter to complete each word.

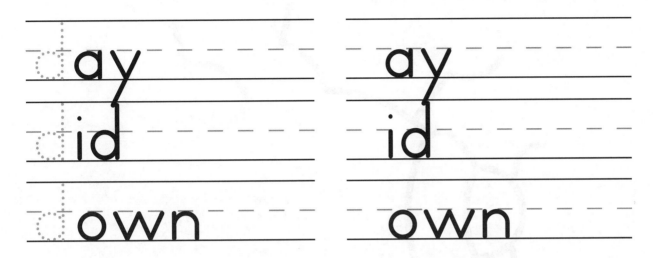

d ay   ay

d id   id

d own   own

Directions: Trace the letters. Then, write the missing letters to complete the sentence.

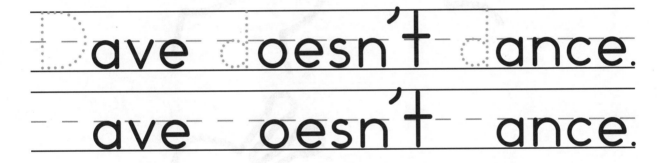

Dave doesn't dance.

ave oesn't ance.

© Shell Education

Name: _____ Date: _____

Directions: Connect the dots. Then, color the pictures.

Activity

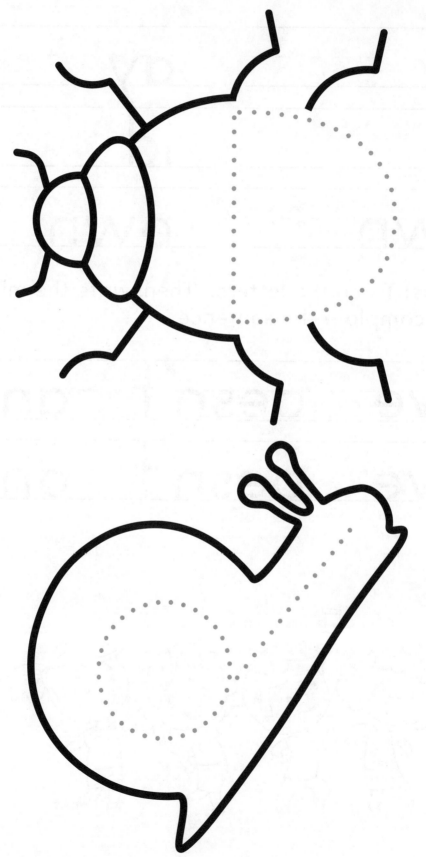

© Shell Education

Name: _____ Date: _____

Directions: Trace each letter. Then, write your own letters to fill the lines.

E _____

e _____

D _____

d _____

Directions: Trace the letters. Then, write the missing letter to complete each word.

ift   ift

oes   oes

nd   nd

Name: _____ Date: _____

Directionality and Strokes

Curve around to the bottom, it's true, that's the way we write the 2!

Directions: Start at each star. Draw each line in the rainbow. Then, color the rainbow.

© Shell Education

Name: _____ Date: _____

2 two

Directions: Trace each number. Then, complete each number.

2 0   0   2 5   5

2 1   2 6   6

2 2   2 7   7

2 3   3   2 8   8

2 4   4   2 9   9

Print Numbers

Name: _____ Date: _____

Directions: Trace each number to complete the math problems.

$2 + 2 = 4$

$20 + 1 = 21$

$22 + 1 = 23$

Directions: Solve each math problem.

$10 + 2 =$ _____

$20 + 2 =$ _____

130194—180 Days of Printing: Advanced   © Shell Education

Sentence Practice

Name: _____ Date: _____

Directions: Connect the dots. Count as you write.
Then, color the picture

Activity

1
2
30   29
31
3   28
5   27
6   4
7   26 •   25
24
8   23
9   10   21   22
11   20
12   19
13   15   16   18
14   17

Name: _____ Date: _____

Directions: Trace each letter and number. Then, write your own letters and numbers to fill the lines.

E

e

D

d

2

Directions: Trace the letters. Then, write the missing letter to complete each word.

d o

d oes

coul d

o

oes

coul

130194—180 Days of Printing: Advanced   © Shell Education

Name: _____ Date: _____

P sits on the line, but *p* goes through it.

Directions: Start at each star. Connect the dots.

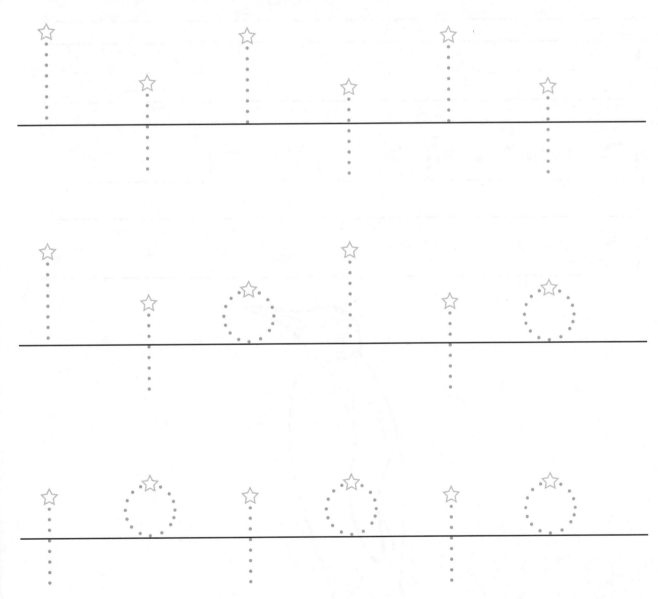

© Shell Education

Name: _____   Date: _____

Directions: Follow the arrows. Trace each letter.
Then, write your own letters to fill the lines

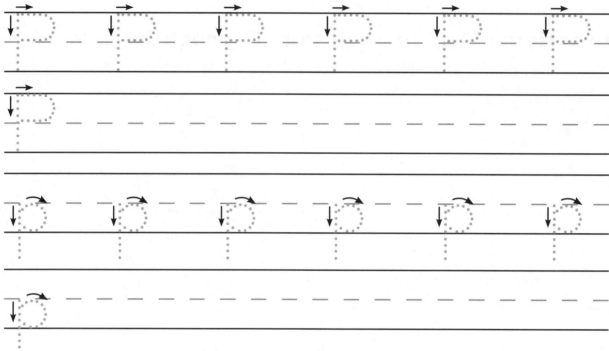

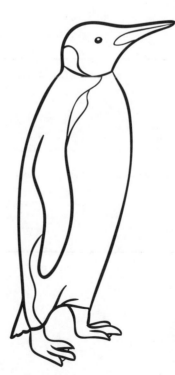

© Shell Education

Name: _____ Date: _____

Directions: Trace the letters. Then, write the missing letter to complete each word.

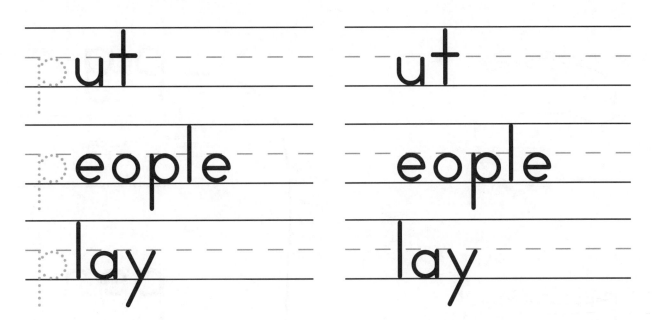

put   ut

people   eople

play   lay

Directions: Trace the letters. Then, write the missing letters to complete the sentence.

Patty plays piano.

atty lays iano.

Name: _____ Date: _____

Directions: Match each word to a picture.
Then, write the words.

Activity

pig

pig

pen

pot

cup

Name: _____ Date: _____

Directions: Trace each letter. Then, write your own letters to fill the lines.

D — — — — — — — — — — — — —

d — — — — — — — — — — — — —

P — — — — — — — — — — — — —

p — — — — — — — — — — — — —

Directions: Trace the letters. Then, write the missing letters to complete the words.

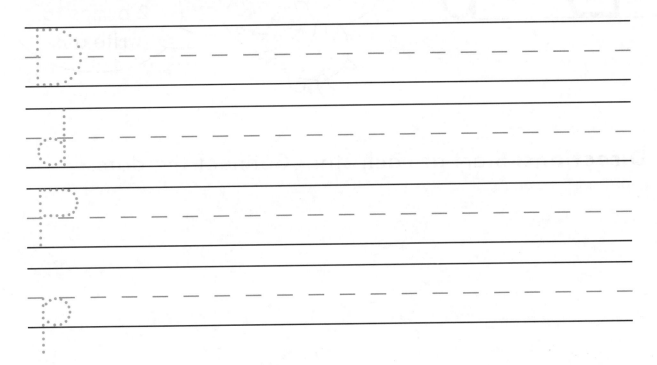

part   art

place   lace

placed   lac

Name: _____ Date: _____

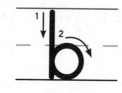

A line and 2 bumps to write a *B*.

Directionality and Strokes

Directions: Start at each star. Connect the dots.

© Shell Education

Name: _____ Date: _____

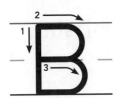 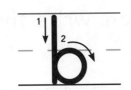

Directions: Follow the arrows. Trace each letter. Then, write your own letters to fill the lines.

© Shell Education

Name: _____ Date: _____

Sentence Practice

Directions: Trace the letters. Then, write the missing letter to complete each word.

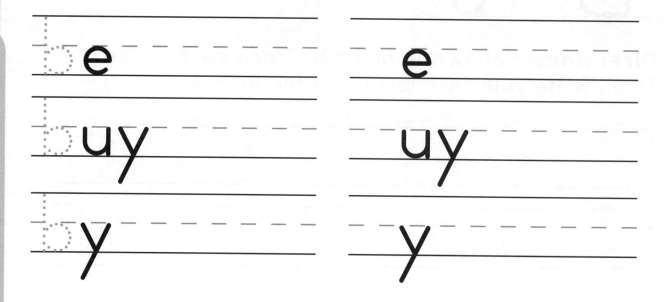

Directions: Trace the letters. Then, write the missing letters to complete the sentence.

© Shell Education

Name: _____ Date: _____

Directions: Color each shape with a *b* blue.
Color the shapes with *p*, *d*, and *a* orange.

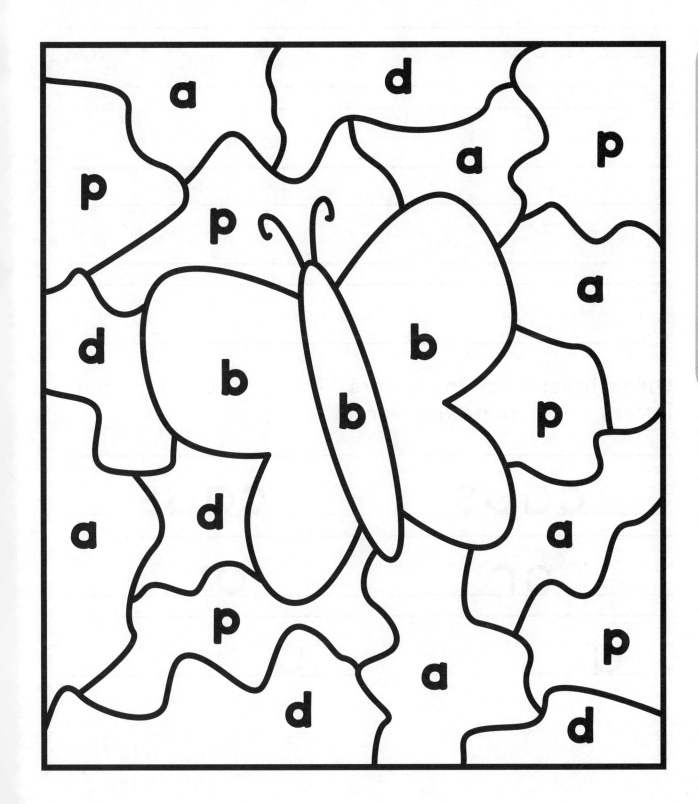

Activity

Name: _____ Date: _____

Directions: Trace each letter. Then, write your own letters to fill the lines.

Review

P

p

B

b

Directions: Trace the letters. Then, write the missing letters to complete the words.

because   caus

before   or

but   u

Name: _____ Date: _____

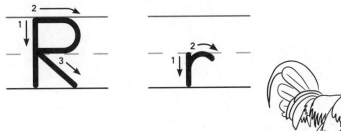

Use curved lines to write *R* and *r*.

Directionality and Strokes

Directions: Start at each star. Connect the dots.

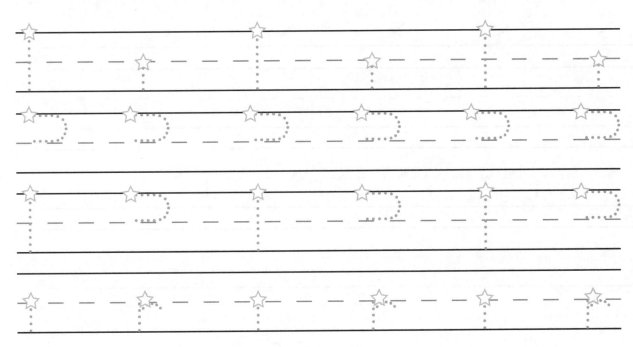

Name: _____ Date: _____

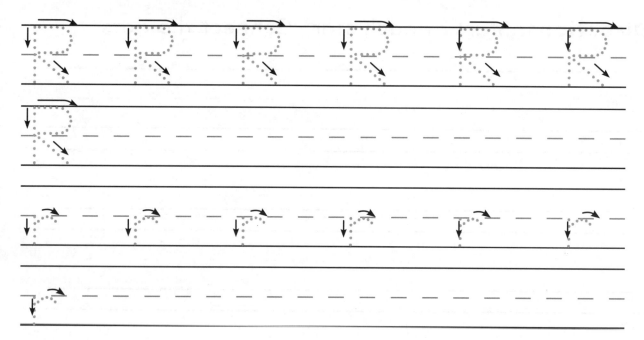

Directions: Follow the arrows. Trace each letter.
Then, write your own letters to fill the lines.

© Shell Education

Print Uppercase and Lowercase

Name: _____ Date: _____

Directions: Trace the letters. Then, write the missing letters to complete the words.

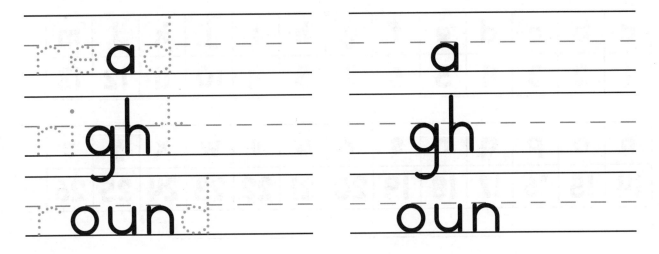

Directions: Trace the letters. Then, write the missing letters to complete the sentence.

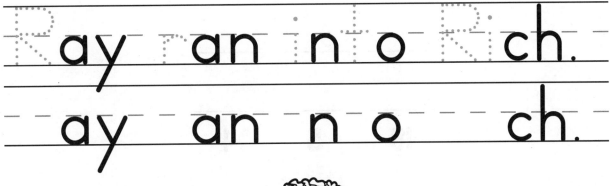

Name: _____ Date: _____

Directions: Use the key. Match the letters to the numbers to write the words.

Activity

a	b	c	d	e	f	g	h	i	j	k	l	m
1	2	3	4	5	6	7	8	9	10	11	12	13

n	o	p	q	r	s	t	u	v	w	x	y	z
14	15	16	17	18	19	20	21	22	23	24	25	26

_____ _____ _____ _____

6   9   18   5

_____ _____ _____

18   5   4

_____ _____ _____ _____

2   9   18   4

_____ _____ _____ _____

20   18   5   5

© Shell Education

Name: _____ Date: _____

Directions: Trace each letter. Then, write your own letters to fill the lines.

B -

b -

R -

r -

Directions: Trace each letter. Then, write the words two more times each.

are -

be -

friend -

Name: _____ Date: _____

Curving twice you can see, that's the way we write the *3*!

Directions: Follow the arrow. Connect the dots.

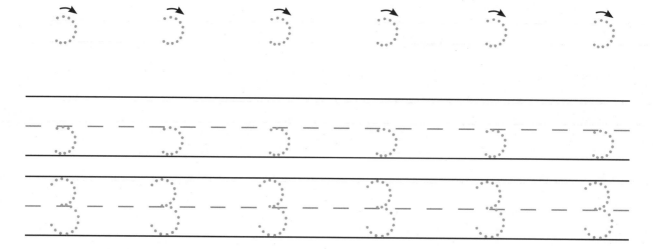

© Shell Education

Directionality and Strokes

Name: _____ Date: _____

3 three

Directions: Trace each number. Then, complete each number.

0   0   5   5

1   6   6

2   7   7

3   8   8

4   4   9   9

Print Numbers

© Shell Education   130194—180 Days of Printing: Advanced   69

Name: _____ Date: _____

Sentence Practice

Directions: Trace each number to complete the math problems.

1 + 2 = 3

10 + 3 = 13

30 + 1 = 31

Directions: Solve each math problem.

3 + 10 = _____

12 + 1 = _____

© Shell Education

Name: _____ Date: _____

Directions: Trace along the dots. Color the picture.

© Shell Education

130194—180 Days of Printing: Advanced

71

Name: _____ Date: _____

Directions: Trace each letter and number. Then, write your own letters and numbers to fill the lines.

R -

r -

P -

p -

3 -

Directions: Trace each letter. Then, write the words two more times each.

a -

at -

the -

Review

© Shell Education

Name: _____ Date: _____

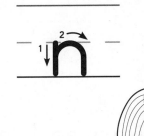

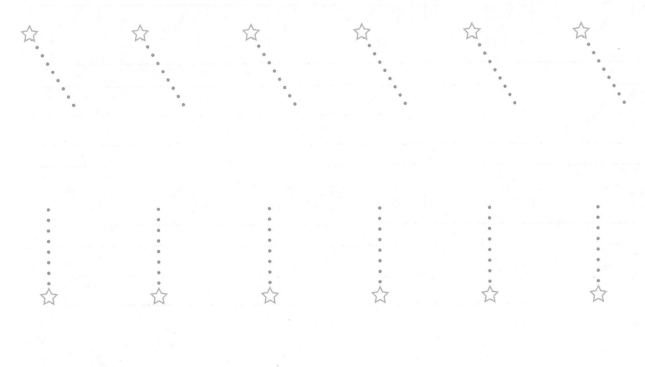

Down and round to make an *n*.

Directionality and Strokes

Directions: Start at each star. Connect the dots.

Name: _____ Date: _____

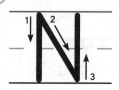 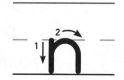

Print Uppercase and Lowercase

Directions: Follow the arrows. Trace each letter. Then, write your own letters to fill the lines.

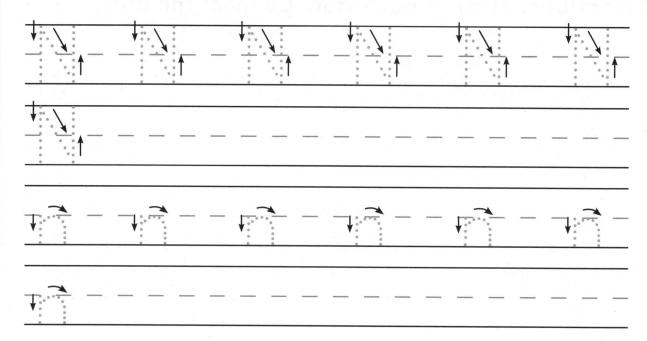

© Shell Education

Name: _____ Date: _____

Directions: Trace the letters. Then, write the missing letters to complete the words.

not | o

now | ow

number | um r

Directions: Trace the letters. Then, write the missing letters to complete the sentence.

Nancy's not

napping now.

a cy's o

app g ow.

Name: _____ Date: _____

Directions: Use the picture clues to complete the crossword puzzle.

Review

1 Down

2 Down

1 Across

3 Across

4 Across

Name: _____ Date: _____

Directions: Trace each letter. Then, write your own letters to fill the lines.

i

i

i

i

Directions: Trace each letter. Then, write the words two more times each.

all

am

and

Name: _____ Date: _____

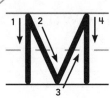 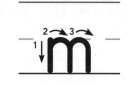 

Practice, practice *M* and *m*.

Directionality and Strokes

Directions: Start at each star. Connect the dots.

© Shell Education

Name: _____ Date: _____

Directions: Follow the arrows. Trace each letter. Then, write your own letters to fill the lines.

Name: _____ Date: _____

Sentence Practice

Directions: Trace the letters. Then, write the missing letters to complete the words.

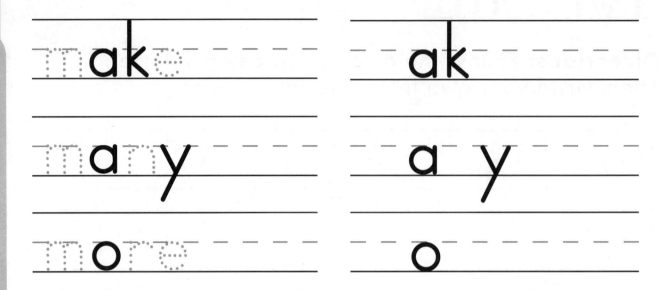

Directions: Trace the letters. Then, write the missing letters to complete the sentence.

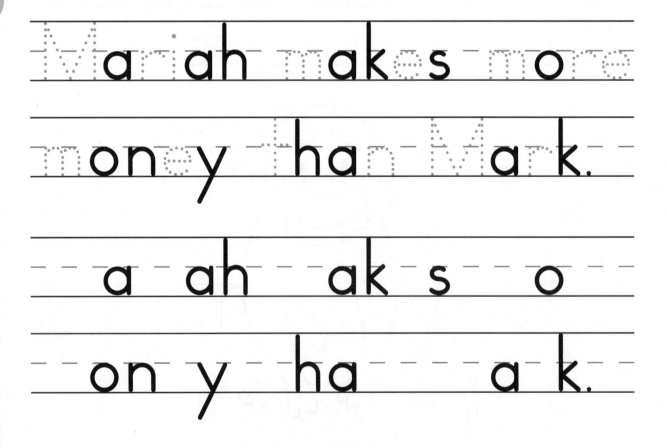

© Shell Education

Name: _____ Date: _____

Directions: Use straight lines to finish the maze.

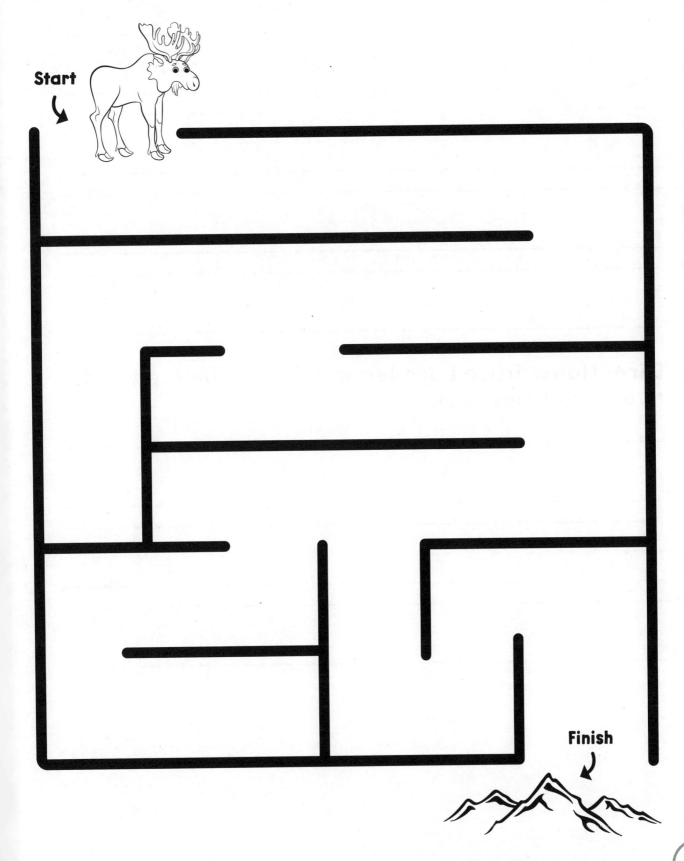

Start

Finish

Name: _____ Date: _____

Review

Directions: Trace each letter. Then, write your own letters to fill the lines.

N

n

M

m

Directions: Trace each letter. Then, write the words two more times each.

are

at

been

© Shell Education

Name: _____ Date: _____

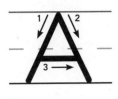

Down, down, and line across to write A.

Directionality and Strokes

Directions: Start at each star. Connect the dots.

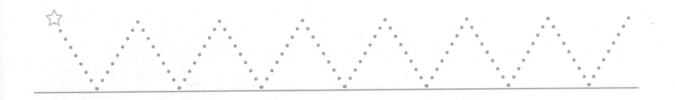

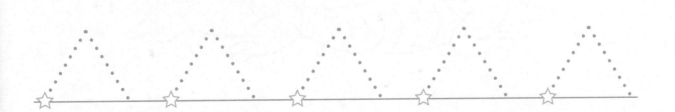

Name: _____   Date: _____

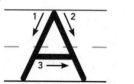 

Directions: Follow the arrows. Trace each letter. Then, write your own letters to fill the lines.

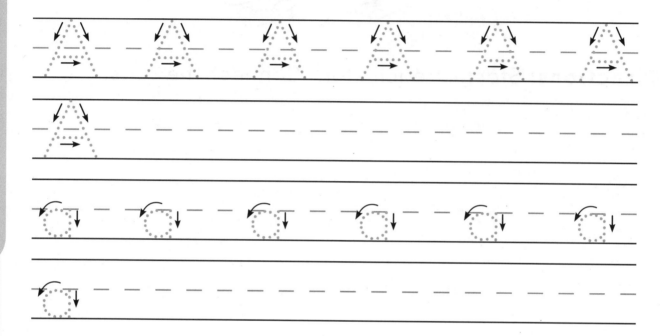

    © Shell Education

Name: _____ Date: _____

Directions: Trace the letters. Then, write the missing letters to complete the words.

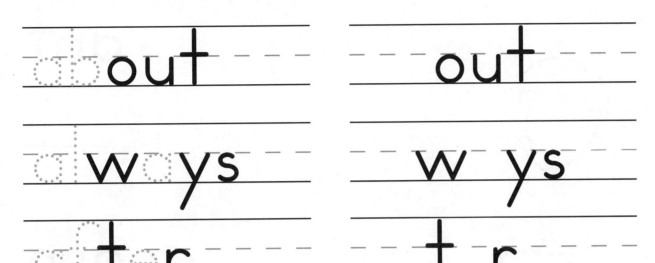

Directions: Trace the letters. Then, write the missing letters to complete the sentence.

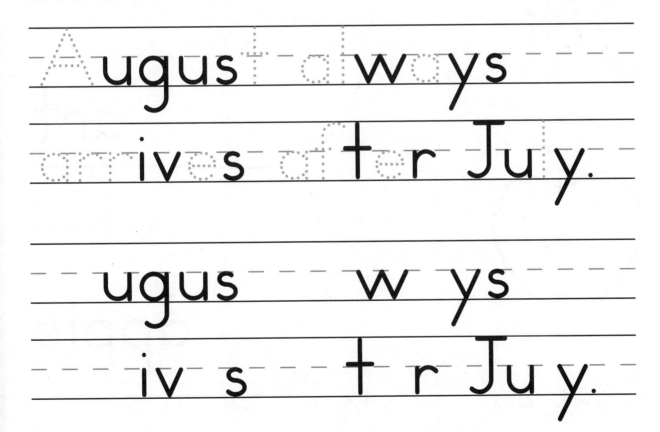

Sentence Practice

Name: _____ Date: _____

Directions: Match each word to a picture.
Then, write the words.

Activity

ant

_____
- - - - - - - - -
_____

acorn

_____
- - - - - - - - -
_____

art

_____
- - - art - - -
_____

apple

_____
- - - - - - - - -
_____

© Shell Education

Name: _____ Date: _____

Directions: Trace each letter. Then, write your own letters to fill the lines.

M _____

m _____

A _____

a _____

Review

Directions: Trace each letter. Then, write the words two more times each.

made _____

man _____

me _____

Name: _____ Date: _____

Down, right, then to the floor, that's the way we write the 4!

Directionality and Strokes

Directions: Start at each star. Connect the dots.

© Shell Education

Name: _____ Date: _____

4 four

Directions: Trace each number. Then, complete each number.

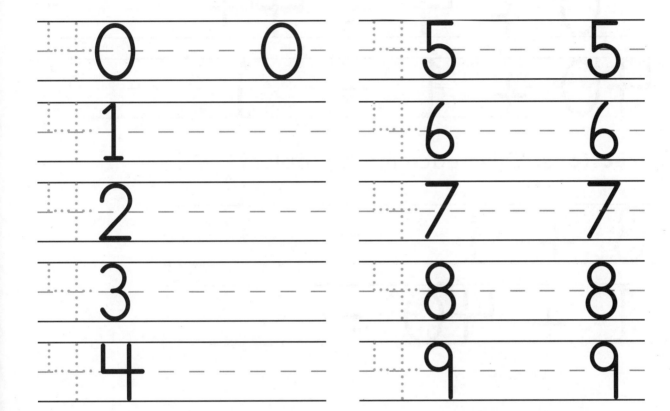

© Shell Education 130194—180 Days of Printing: Advanced

Name: _____ Date: _____

Directions: Trace each number to complete the math problems.

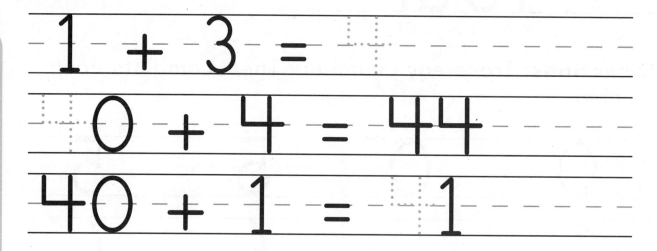

$1 + 3 =$

$0 + 4 = 44$

$40 + 1 = 1$

Directions: Solve each math problem.

$3 + 1 = $ _____

$1 + 40 = $ _____

© Shell Education

Name: _____ Date: _____

Directions: Count the items. Tally as you count. Then, write the numbers.

Count	Tally Mark	Number
	‖‖	4

© Shell Education

Name: _____ Date: _____

Review

Directions: Trace each letter or number. Then, write your own letters or numbers to fill the lines.

M

m

A

a

4

Directions: Trace each letter. Then, write the words two more times each.

an

land

man

© Shell Education

Name: _____ Date: _____

One line down and a hump to write an *h*.

Directions: Start at each star. Connect the dots.

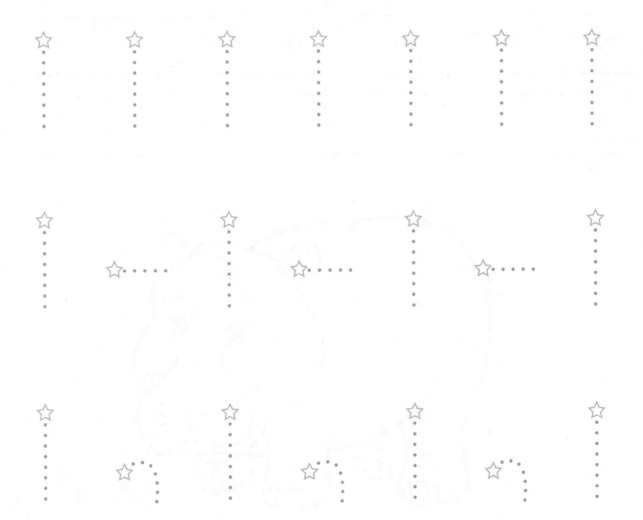

Name: _____ Date: _____

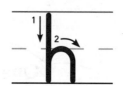

Directions: Follow the arrows. Trace each letter. Then, write your own letters to fill the lines.

© Shell Education

Name: _____ Date: _____

Directions: Trace the letters. Then, write the missing letters to complete the words.

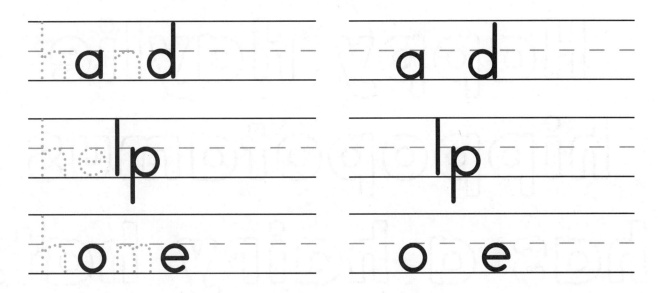

Sentence Practice

Directions: Trace the letters. Then, write the missing letters to complete the sentence.

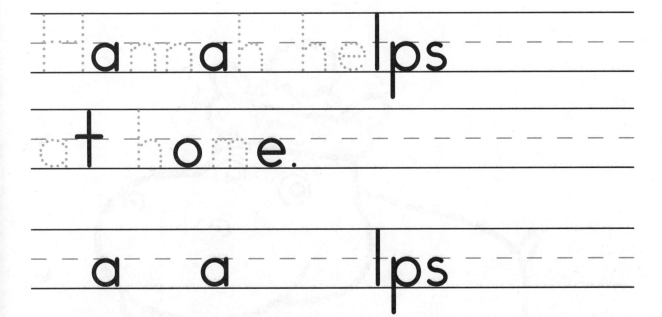

Name: _____ Date: _____

Directions: Read the tongue twister. Circle each *H* and underline each *h*. Then, color the picture.

Happy Haylie hippopotamus has a hairy hat.

130194—180 Days of Printing: Advanced

© Shell Education

Name: _____ Date: _____

Directions: Trace each letter. Then, write your own letters to fill the lines.

A

a

H

h

Directions: Trace each letter. Then, write the words two more times each.

he

her

them

Name: _____ Date: _____

One line down, then in and out. That's the way to make a *K*.

Directionality and Strokes

Directions: Start at each star. Connect the dots.

© Shell Education

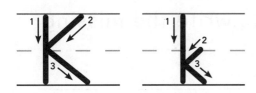

Directions: Follow the arrows. Trace each letter.
Then, write your own letters to fill the lines.

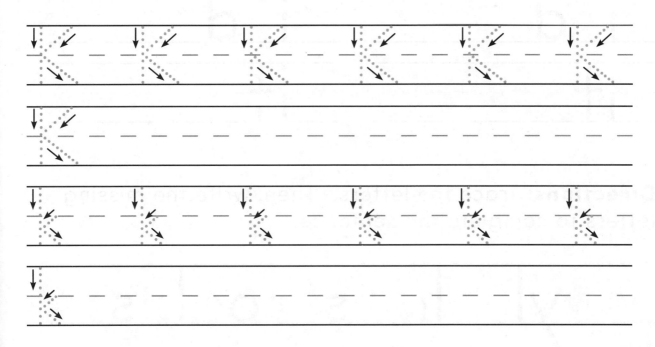

Name: _____ Date: _____

Sentence Practice

Directions: Trace the letters. Then, write the missing letters to complete the words.

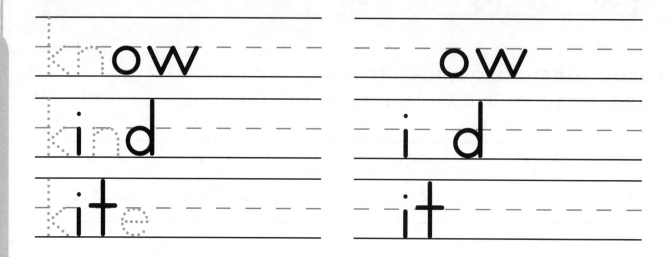

Directions: Trace the letters. Then, write the missing letters to complete the sentence.

© Shell Education

Name: _____ Date: _____

Directions: Use the picture clues to complete the crossword puzzle.

1 Down

2 Down

1 Across

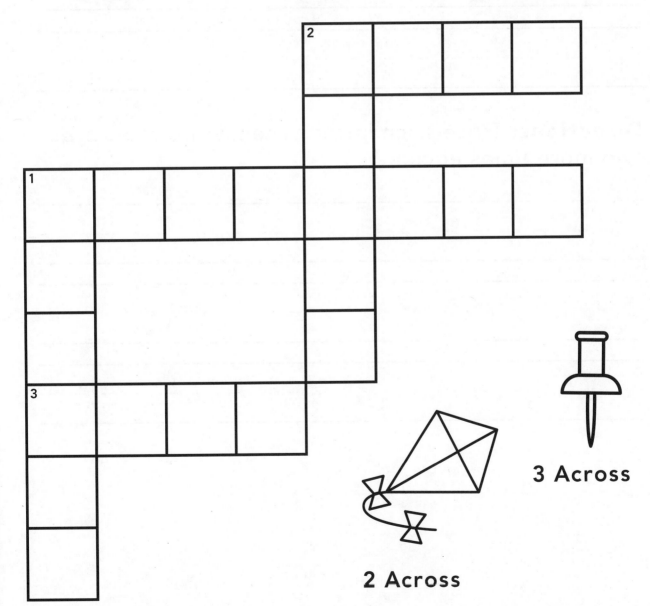

3 Across

2 Across

© Shell Education

Activity

Name: _____ Date: _____

Review

Directions: Trace each letter. Then, write your own letters to fill the lines.

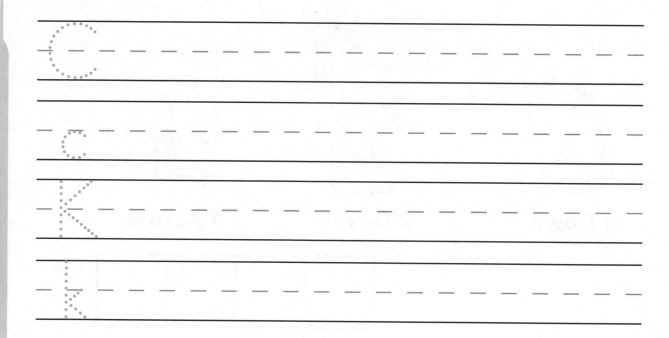

Directions: Trace each letter. Then, write the words two more times each.

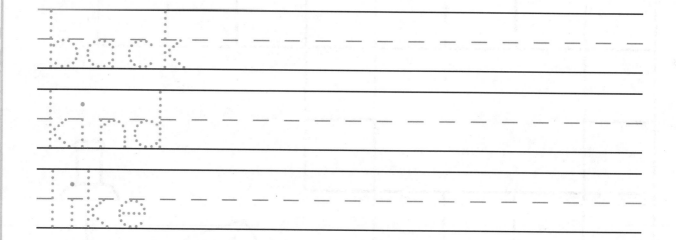

    © Shell Education

Name: _____ Date: _____

Down and around then back up to the right, that's the way we write the 5!

Directions: Start at each star. Connect the dots.

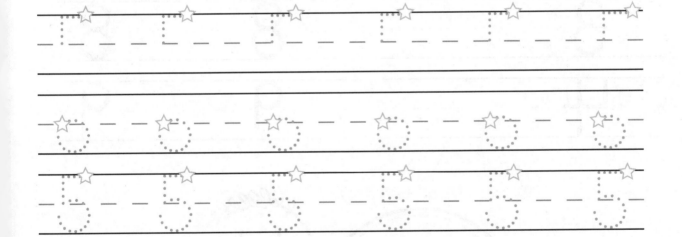

Name: _____ Date: _____

3 →
1 ↓ 2
5 five

Directions: Trace each number. Then, complete each number.

Print Numbers

5 0   0   5 5

5 1   5 6   6

5 2   5 7   7

5 3   5 8   8

5 4   5 9   9

© Shell Education

Name: _____ Date: _____

Directions: Trace each number to complete the math problems.

$$1 + 4 = 5$$

$$10 + 5 = 15$$

$$50 + 1 = 51$$

Directions: Solve each math problem.

$$5 + 10 = \underline{\qquad}$$

$$1 + 50 = \underline{\qquad}$$

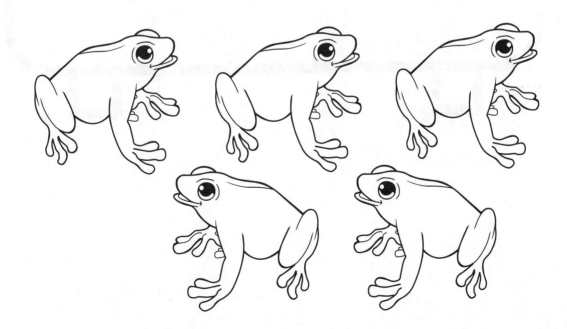

© Shell Education

Name: _____ Date: _____

Directions: Connect the dots. Draw 5 circles on the chair. Then, color the picture.

Activity

© Shell Education

Name: _____ Date: _____

Directions: Trace each letter or number. Then, write your own letters and numbers to fill the lines.

C -

c -

H -

h -

5 -

Directions: Trace each letter. Then, write the words two more times each.

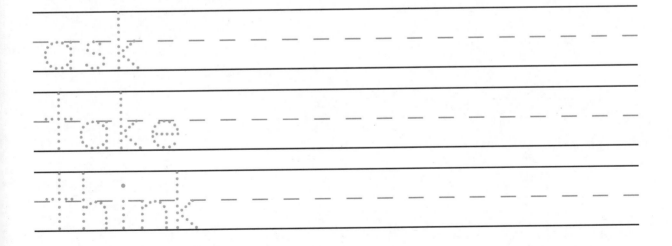

ask -

take -

think -

Name: _____ Date: _____

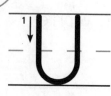

Down, round,
and up to
make a *U*.

Directionality and Strokes

Directions: Start at each star. Connect the dots.

© Shell Education

Name: _____ Date: _____

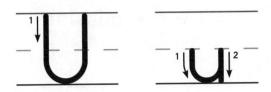

Directions: Follow the arrows. Trace each letter. Then, write your own letters to fill the lines

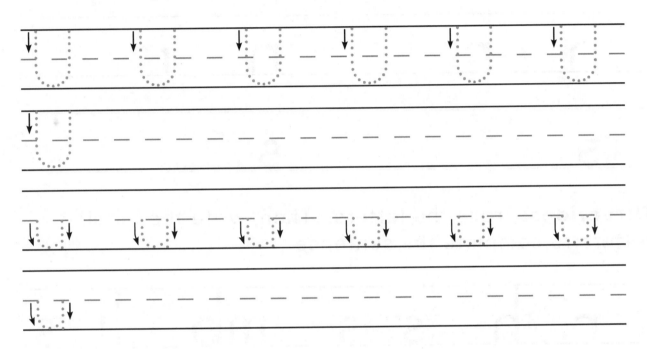

Name: _____ Date: _____

Directions: Trace the letters. Then, write the missing letters to complete the words.

Sentence Practice

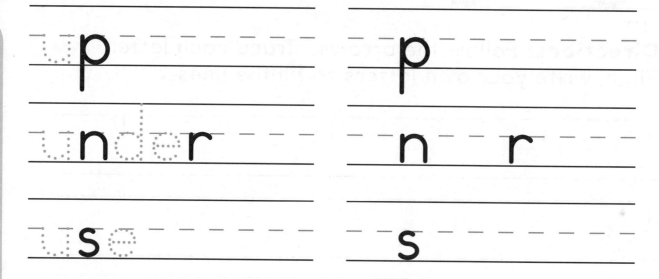

Directions: Trace the letters. Then, write the missing letters to complete the sentence.

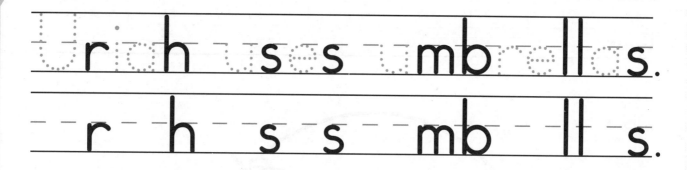

© Shell Education

Name: _____ Date: _____

Directions: Match the letters to the numbers. Find the answer to the riddle.

What goes up when rain comes down?

a	b	c	d	e	f	g	h	i	j	k	l	m
1	2	3	4	5	6	7	8	9	10	11	12	13

n	o	p	q	r	s	t	u	v	w	x	y	z
14	15	16	17	18	19	20	21	22	23	24	25	26

_____ _____
1   14

_____ _____ _____ _____ _____ _____ _____ _____
21   13   2   18   5   12   12   1

Name: _____ Date: _____

Directions: Trace each letter. Then, write your own letters to fill the lines.

Review

I

i

H

h

Directions: Trace each letter. Then, write the words two more times each.

much

turn

animal

Name: _____ Date: _____

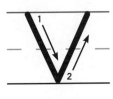

One line down and one line up, you see. That's the way you write a *V*.

Directions: Start at each star. Connect the dots.

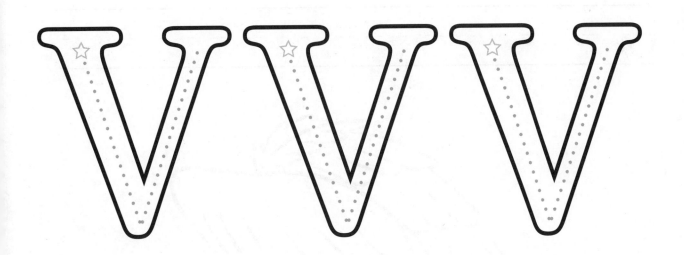

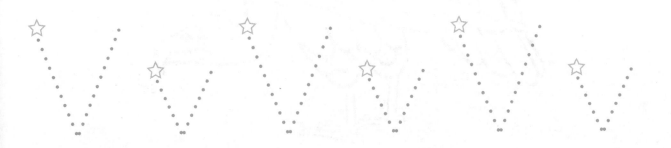

Name: _____ Date: _____

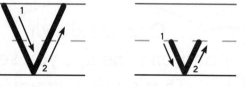

Directions: Follow the arrows. Trace each letter. Then, write your own letters to fill the lines.

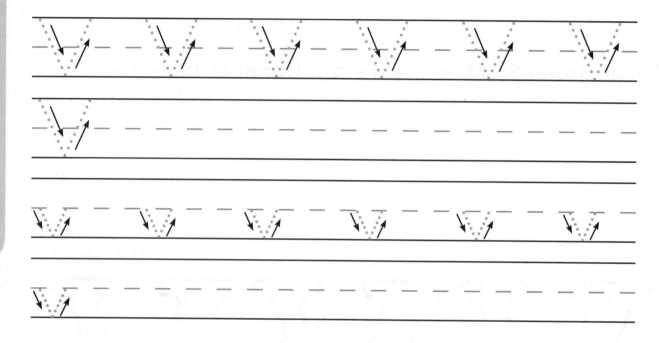

130194—180 Days of Printing: Advanced   © Shell Education

Name: _____ Date: _____

Directions: Trace the letters. Then, write the missing letters to complete the words.

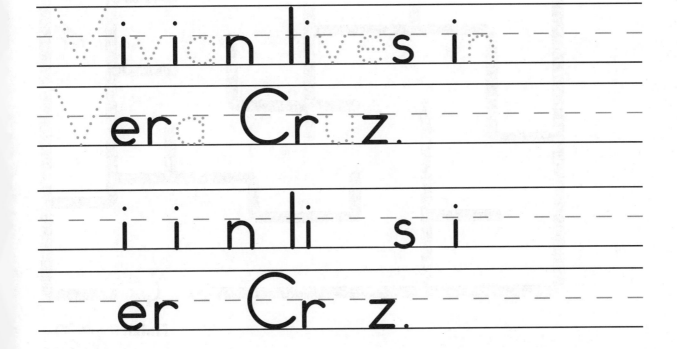

ey   ey

ae   ae

ie   ie

Directions: Trace the letters. Then, write the missing letters to complete the sentence.

Vivian lives in

Vera Cruz.

i i n li si

er Cr z.

© Shell Education   130194—180 Days of Printing: Advanced   115

Name: _____ Date: _____

Directions: Use straight lines to complete the maze.

Activity

Start

Finish

© Shell Education

Name: _____ Date: _____

Directions: Trace each letter. Then, write your own letters to fill the lines.

U

u

V

v

Directions: Trace each letter. Then, write the words two more times each.

have

live

very

© Shell Education

Name: _____ Date: _____

Down and around, no need for tricks, that's the way we write the 6!

Directions: Start at each star. Connect the dots.

© Shell Education

Name: _____ Date: _____

6 six

Directions: Follow the arrows. Trace each number. Then, write your own numbers to fill the lines.

Name: _____ Date: _____

Directions: Trace each number to complete the math problems.

$$1 + 5 = 6$$

$$11 + 5 = 16$$

$$60 + 1 = 61$$

Directions: Solve each math problem.

$$6 + 10 = \underline{\hspace{2cm}}$$

$$1 + 60 = \underline{\hspace{2cm}}$$

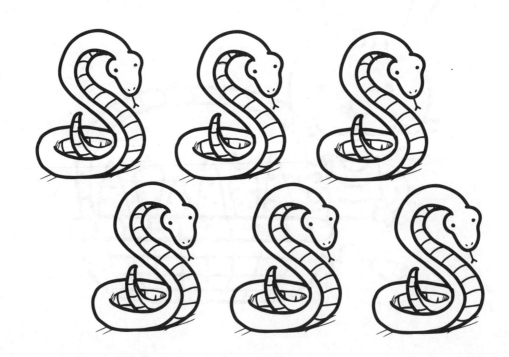

© Shell Education

Sentence Practice

Name: _____ Date: _____

Directions: Trace along the dots. Color the picture.

Name: _____ Date: _____

Directions: Trace each letter and number. Then, write your own letters and numbers to fill the lines.

Review

U — — — — — — — — — — — — — —

u — — — — — — — — — — — — — —

Y — — — — — — — — — — — — — —

y — — — — — — — — — — — — — —

6 — — — — — — — — — — — — — —

Directions: Trace each letter. Then, write the words two more times each.

have — — — — — — — — — —

every — — — — — — — — — —

even — — — — — — — — — —

       © Shell Education

Name: _____ Date: _____

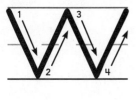

Diagonal lines are mighty fine.

Directions: Start at each star. Connect the dots.

Name: _____ Date: _____

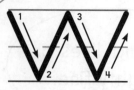 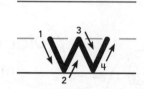

Print Uppercase and Lowercase

Directions: Follow the arrows. Trace each letter. Then, write your own letters to fill the lines.

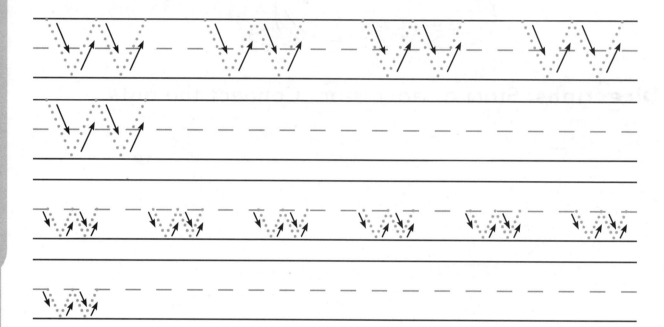

© Shell Education

Name: _____ Date: _____

Sentence Practice

Directions: Trace the letters. Then, write the missing letters to complete the words.

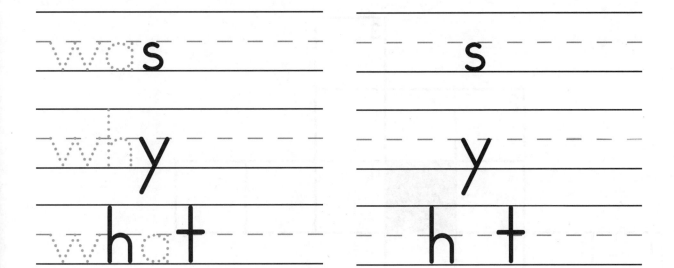

Directions: Trace the letters. Then, write the missing letters to complete the sentence.

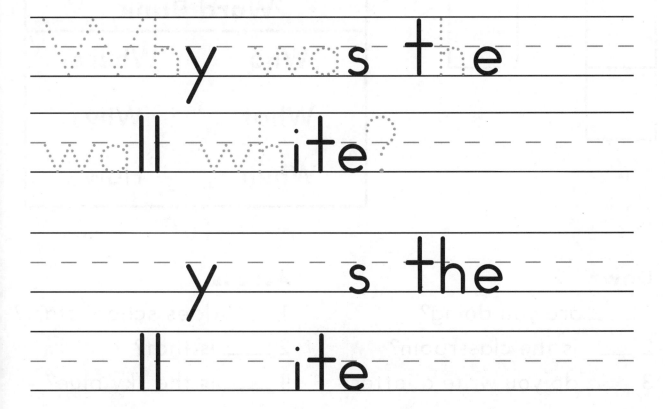

© Shell Education

Name: _____ Date: _____

Directions: Finish the questions to complete the crossword puzzle. Use the word bank to help you.

Activity

Word Bank	
Who	Where
What	Why
When	How

Down

1 ____ are you doing?

2 ____ is the classroom?

3 ____ do you write a letter?

Across

1 ____ does school start?

2 ____ is that?

4 ____ is the sky blue?

Name: _____ Date: _____

Directions: Trace each letter. Then, write your own letters to fill the lines.

V

v

W

w

Directions: Trace each letter. Then, write the words two more times each.

want

what

water

Name: _____ Date: _____

Cross the lines to make an *X*.

Directionality and Strokes

Directions: Start at each star. Connect the dots.

© Shell Education

Name: _____ Date: _____

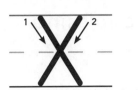 

Directions: Follow the arrows. Trace each letter. Then, write your own letters to fill the lines

Print Uppercase and Lowercase

Name: _____ Date: _____

Sentence Practice

Directions: Trace the letters. Then, write the missing letters to complete the words.

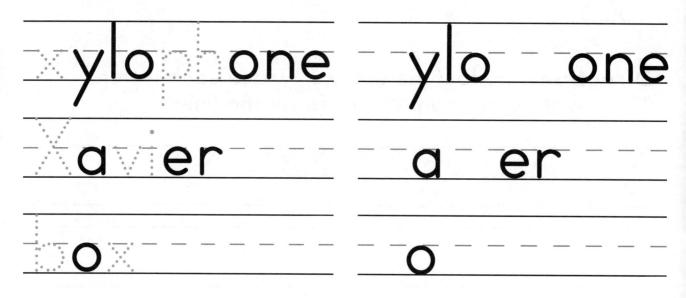

Directions: Trace the letters. Then, write the missing letters to complete the sentence.

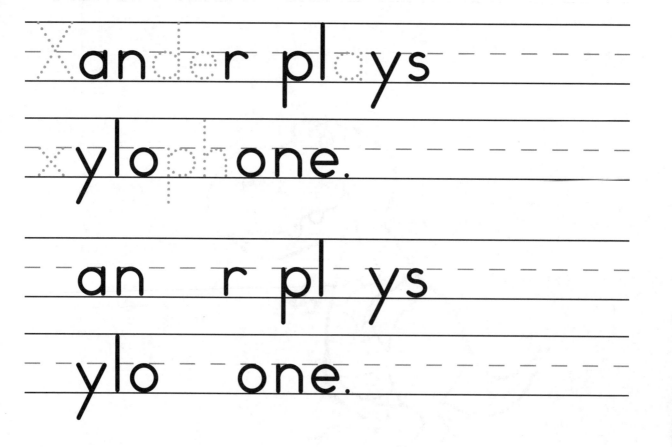

© Shell Education

Name: _____ Date: _____

Directions: Write an X on your favorite foods.
Then, color the picture.

© Shell Education

Name: _____ Date: _____

Review

Directions: Trace each letter. Then, write your own letters to fill the lines.

Y

y

X

x

Directions: Trace each letter. Then, write the words two more times each.

upon

use

went

Name: _____ Date: _____

Top to bottom, left to right, that's the way we write, write, write!

Directions: Start at each star. Connect the dots.

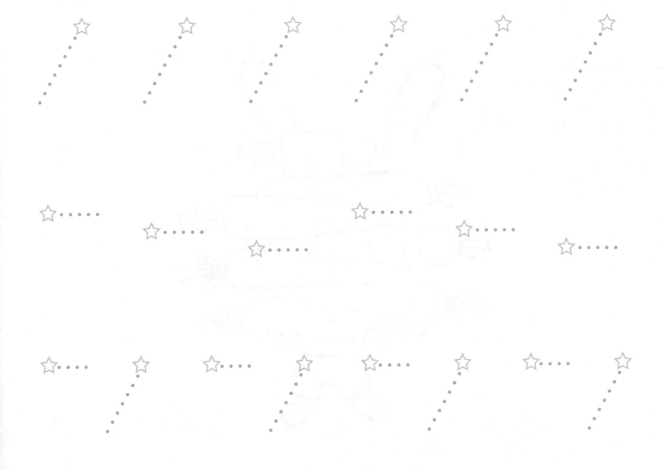

Name: _____ Date: _____

7 seven

Directions: Follow the arrows. Trace each number. Then, write your own numbers to fill the lines.

Print Numbers

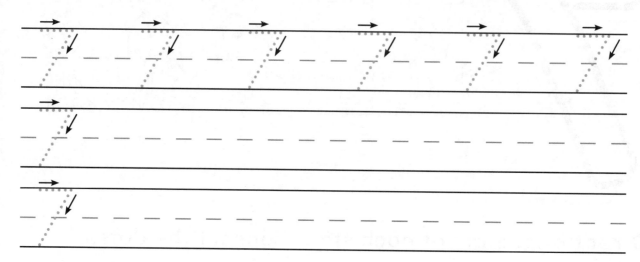

© Shell Education

Name: _____ Date: _____

Directions: Trace each number to complete the math problems.

$1 + 6 = 7$

$10 + 7 = 17$

$70 + 1 = 71$

Directions: Solve each math problem.

$7 + 10 = $ _____

$1 + 70 = $ _____

Name: _____ Date: _____

Activity

Directions: Color the shapes with 7 yellow.
Then, color the shapes with other numbers blue.

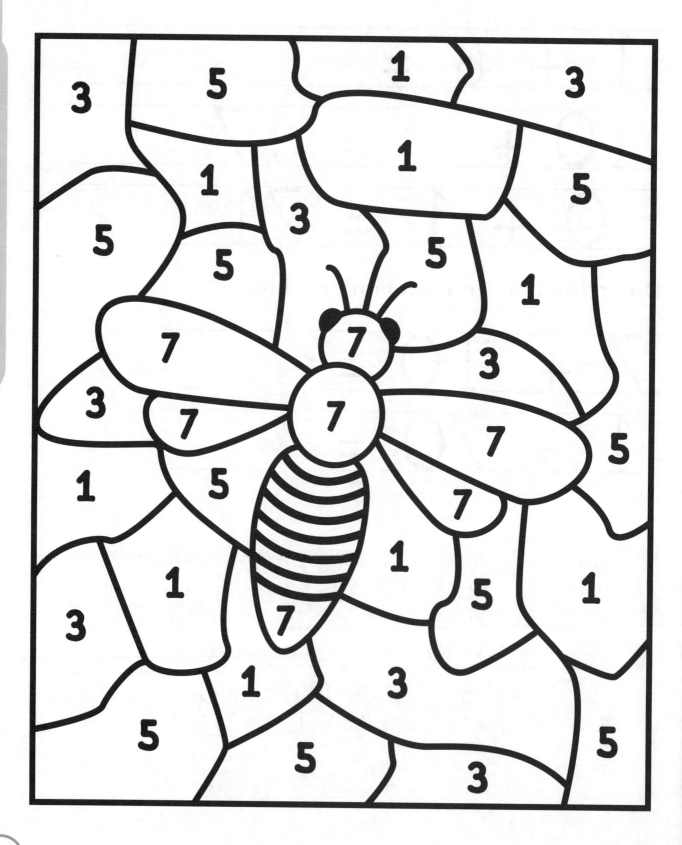

130194—180 Days of Printing: Advanced   © Shell Education

Name: _____ Date: _____

Directions: Trace each letter and number. Then, write your own letters and numbers to fill the lines.

X

x

W

w

7

Directions: Trace each letter. Then, write the words two more times each.

well

went

where

© Shell Education

Review

Name: _____ Date: _____

Directionality and Strokes

Diagonal lines. That's the way to write a y.

Directions: Start at each star. Connect the dots.

© Shell Education

Name: _____ Date: _____

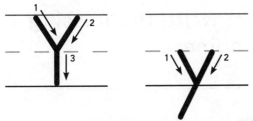

Directions: Follow the arrows. Trace each letter. Then, write your own letters to fill the lines

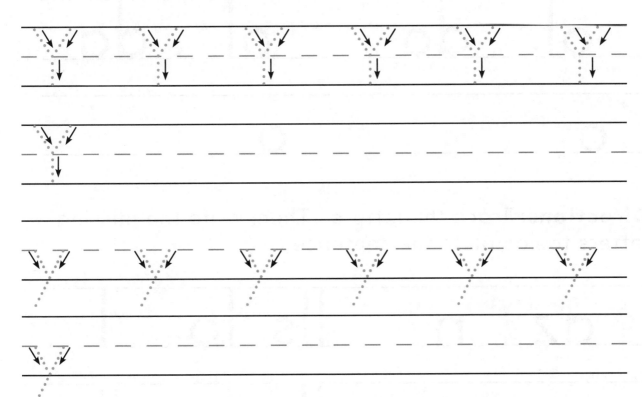

Name: _____ Date: _____

Directions: Trace the letters. Then, write the missing letters to complete the words and name.

Sentence Practice

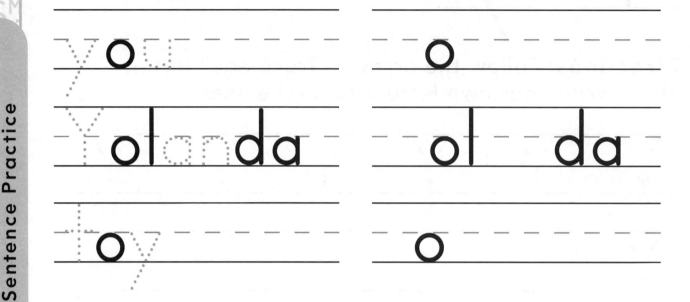

Directions: Trace the letters. Then, write the missing letters to complete the sentence.

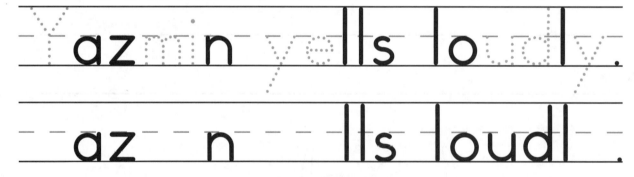

Name: _____ Date: _____

Directions: Use the key. Match the letters to the numbers to answer the riddle.

I am little. There are two of me on your face.
I see everything. What am I?

a	b	c	d	e	f	g	h	i	j	k	l	m
1	2	3	4	5	6	7	8	9	10	11	12	13

n	o	p	q	r	s	t	u	v	w	x	y	z
14	15	16	17	18	19	20	21	22	23	24	25	26

__ __   __ __ __

1   14   5   25   5

Activity

Name: _____ Date: _____

Review

Directions: Trace each letter. Then, write your own letters to fill the lines.

X

x

Y

y

Directions: Trace each letter. Then, write the words two more times each.

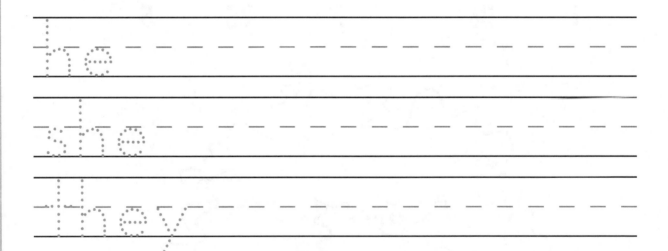

he

she

they

    © Shell Education

Name: _____ Date: _____

Practice writing Z, Z, Z.

Directions: Start at each star. Connect the dots.

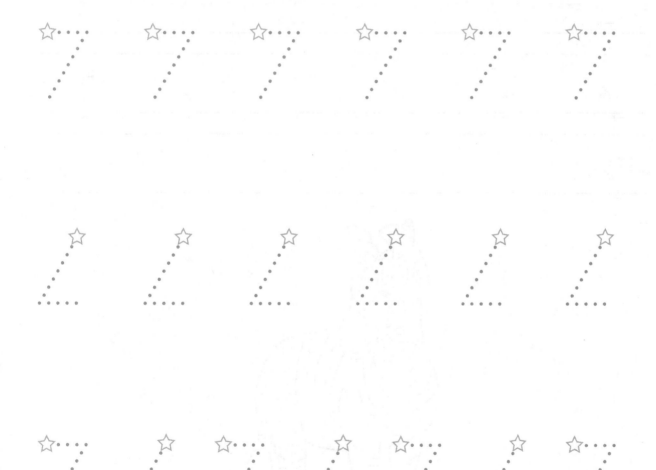

Name: _____ Date: _____

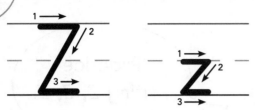

Print Uppercase and Lowercase

Directions: Follow the arrows. Trace each letter.
Then, write your own letters to fill the lines.

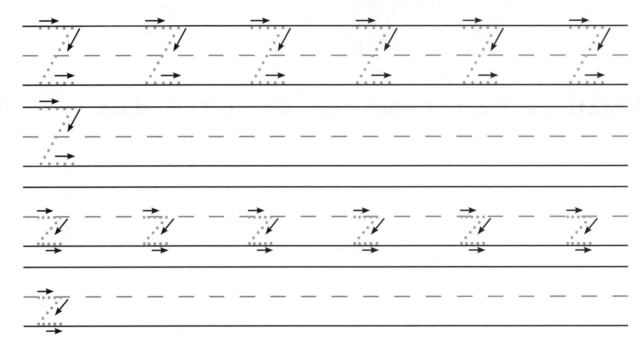

130194—180 Days of Printing: Advanced   © Shell Education

Name: _____ Date: _____

Directions: Trace the letters. Then, write the missing letters to complete the words and name.

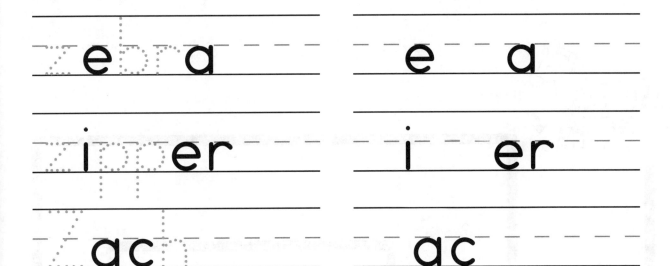

Directions: Trace the letters. Then, write the missing letters to complete the sentence.

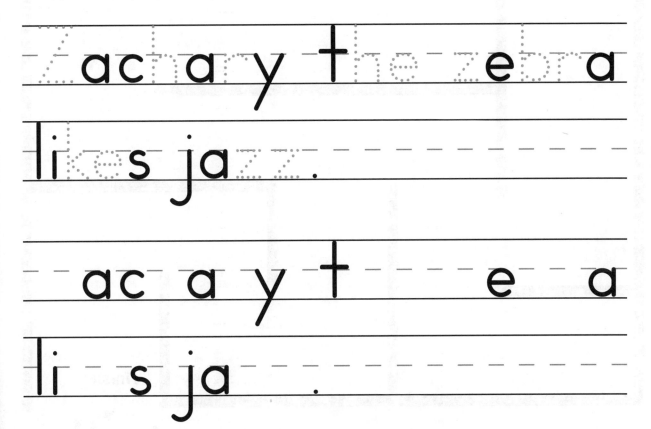

© Shell Education

Name: _____ Date: _____

Directions: Use straight lines to complete the maze.

Activity

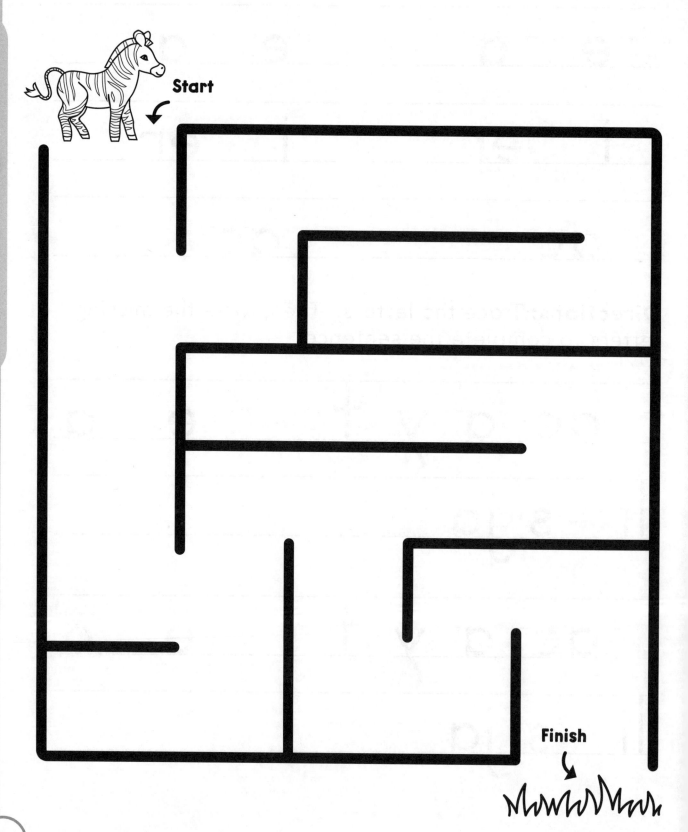

Start

Finish

© Shell Education

Name: _____ Date: _____

Directions: Trace each letter. Then, write your own letters to fill the lines.

Y _____

y _____

Z _____

z _____

Directions: Trace each letter. Then, write the words two more times each.

what _____

why _____

where _____

© Shell Education

Name: _____ Date: _____

Directionality and Strokes

Curve around twice, that looks great. That's the way we write the 8!

Directions: Start at each star. Connect the dots.

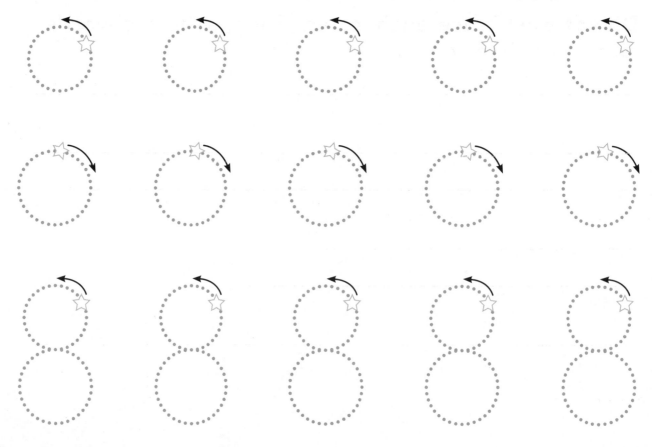

© Shell Education

Name: _____ Date: _____

8 eight

Directions: Trace each number. Then, complete each number.

0   0

1

2

3

4

5

6

7

8

9   9

© Shell Education

Name: _____ Date: _____

Sentence Practice

Directions: Trace each number to complete the math problems.

$$1 + 7 = 8$$

$$80 + 1 = 81$$

$$10 + 8 = 18$$

Directions: Solve each math problem.

$$8 + 10 = \underline{\hspace{2cm}}$$

$$81 + 1 = \underline{\hspace{2cm}}$$

© Shell Education

Name: _____ Date: _____

Directions: Trace along the dots. Then, color the design.

Name: _____ Date: _____

Directions: Trace each letter and number. Then, write your own letters and numbers to fill the lines.

Review

Y

Y

Z

8

Directions: Trace each letter. Then, write the words two more times each.

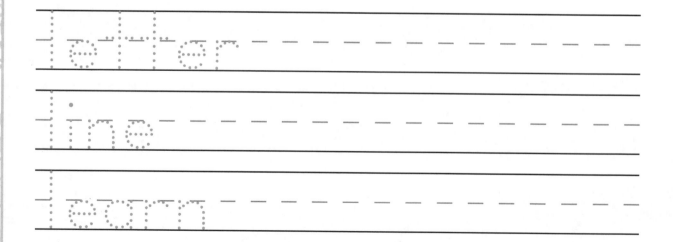

letter

line

learn

© Shell Education

Name: _____ Date: _____

Up and around to write a C.

Directions: Start at each star. Connect the dots. Then, copy the pattern.

Name: _____ Date: _____

Print Uppercase and Lowercase

Directions: Follow the arrows. Trace each letter. Then, write your own letters to fill the lines.

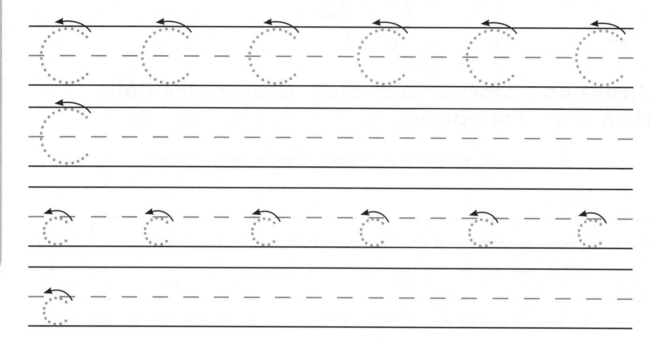

© Shell Education

Name: _____ Date: _____

Directions: Trace the letters. Then, write the missing letters to complete the words.

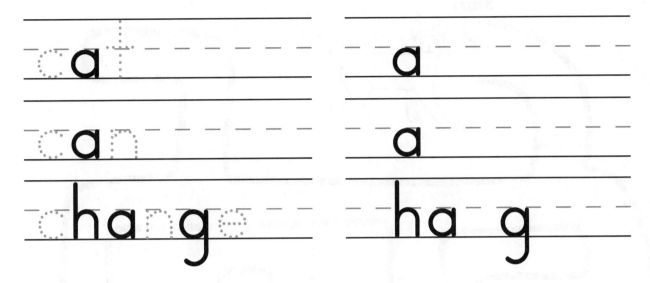

Directions: Trace the letters. Then, write the missing letters to complete the sentence.

© Shell Education

Sentence Practice

Name: _____ Date: _____

Directions: Use curved lines to complete the maze.

Activity

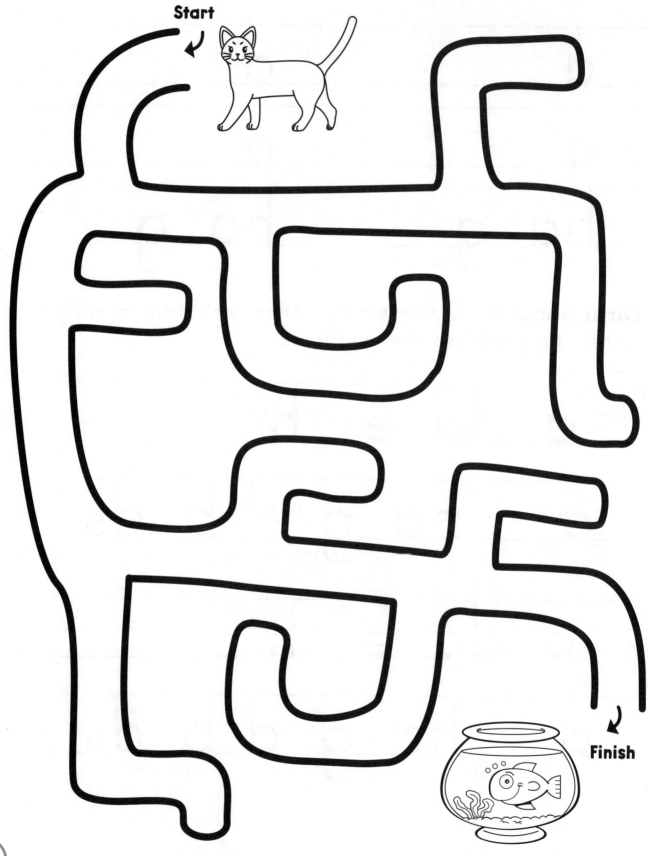

Start

Finish

Name: _____ Date: _____

Directions: Trace each letter. Then, write your own letters to fill the lines.

Z

z

C

c

Directions: Trace each letter. Then, write the words two more times each.

called

which

each

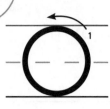

Name: _____ Date: _____

Ollie Octopus writes an O.

Directionality and Strokes

Directions: Start at each star. Trace the circles.

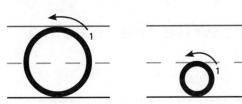

Directions: Follow the arrows. Trace each letter. Then, write your own letters to fill the lines.

Name: _____ Date: _____

Directions: Trace the letters. Then, write the missing letters to complete the words.

Sentence Practice

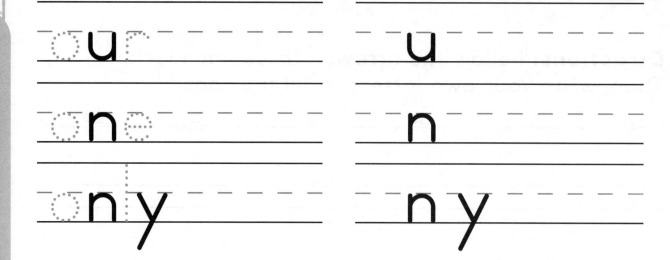

Directions: Trace the letters. Then, write the missing letters to complete the sentence.

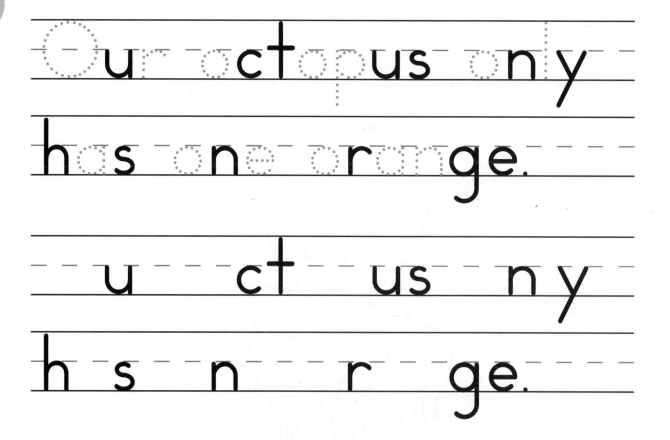

Name: _____ Date: _____

Directions: Circle all the differences in the pictures. How many do you see? Then, color the pictures.

© Shell Education

Activity

Name: _____ Date: _____

Review

Directions: Trace each letter. Then, write your own letters to fill the lines.

C

c

O

o

Directions: Trace each letter. Then, write the words two more times each.

come

could

place

Name: _____ Date: _____

Curve around, drop down, that's fine. That's the way we write the 9!

Directions: Start at each star. Connect the dots.

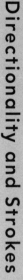

Name: _____ Date: _____

9 nine

Directions: Trace each number. Then, complete each number.

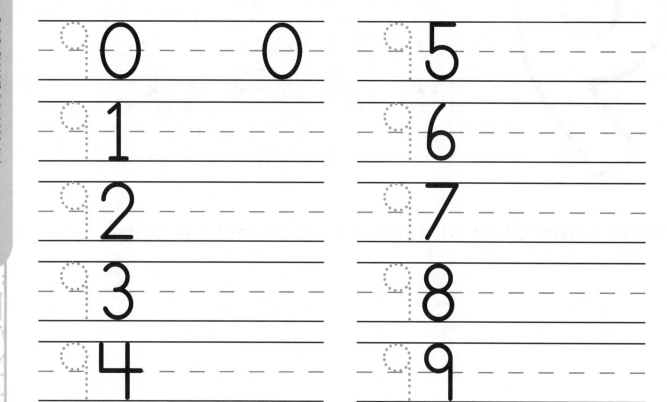

© Shell Education

Name: _____ Date: _____

Directions: Trace each number to complete the math problems.

$$1 + 8 = 9$$

$$0 + 1 = 91$$

$$10 + 9 = 19$$

Directions: Solve each math problem.

$$1 + 90 = \text{\_\_\_\_}$$

$$18 + 1 = \text{\_\_\_\_}$$

Sentence Practice

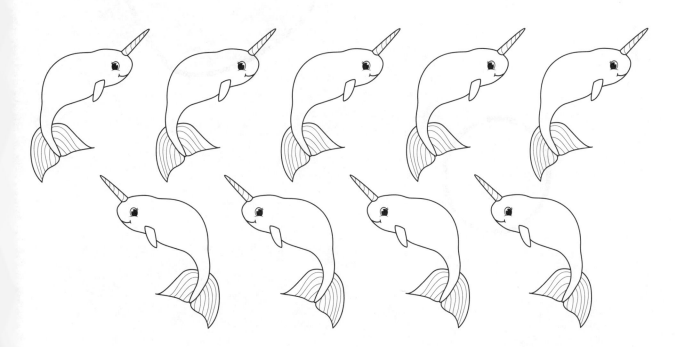

© Shell Education

Name: _____ Date: _____

Directions: Trace along the dots. Color the pictures.

Activity

© Shell Education

Name: _____ Date: _____

Directions: Trace each letter or number. Then, write your own letters and numbers to fill the lines.

C — — — — — — — — — — — — — — — — — —

c — — — — — — — — — — — — — — — — — —

O — — — — — — — — — — — — — — — — — —

o — — — — — — — — — — — — — — — — — —

9 — — — — — — — — — — — — — — — — — —

Directions: Trace each letter. Then, write the words on your own.

each — — — — — — — — — — — — — — — —

came — — — — — — — — — — — — — — — —

change — — — — — — — — — — — — — —

© Shell Education

Review

Name: _____ Date: _____

Circle, line. Circle, line. Writing *Q* is mighty fine.

Directionality and Strokes

Directions: Start at each star. Connect the dots. Then, write your own pattern

© Shell Education

Name: _____ Date: _____

Directions: Follow the arrows. Trace each letter. Then, write your own letters to fill the lines.

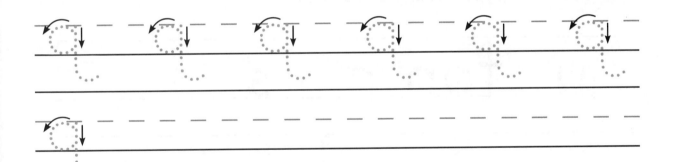

Name: _____ Date: _____

Directions: Trace the letters. Then, write the missing letters to complete the words.

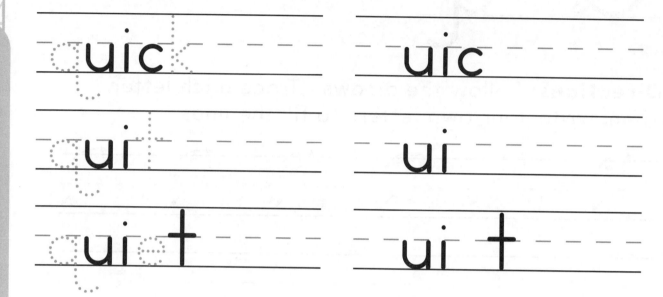

Directions: Trace the letters. Then, write the missing letters to complete the sentence.

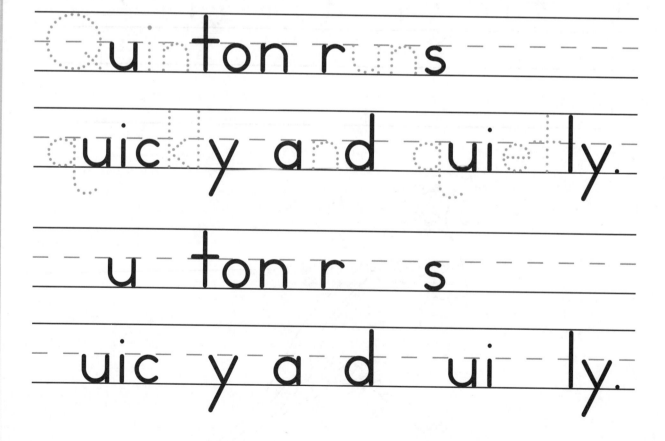

© Shell Education

Name: _____ Date: _____

Directions: Match each word to a picture.
Then, write the words.

quail
_____
- - - - - - - - -
_____

question
_____
- - - - - - - - -
_____

queen
_____
- - - - - - - - -
_____

quilt
_____
- - - - - - - - -
_____

© Shell Education

Name: _____ Date: _____

Review

Directions: Trace each letter. Then, write your own letters to fill the lines.

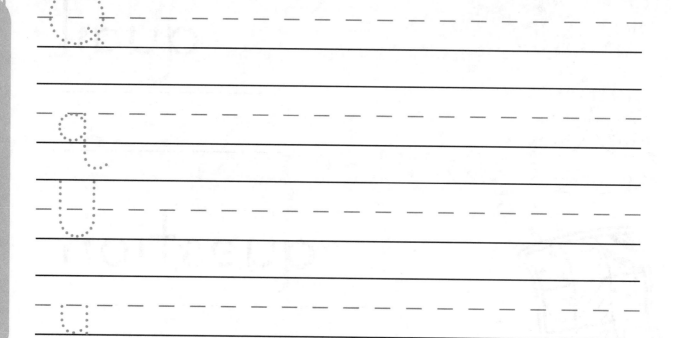

Directions: Trace each letter. Then, write the words two more times each.

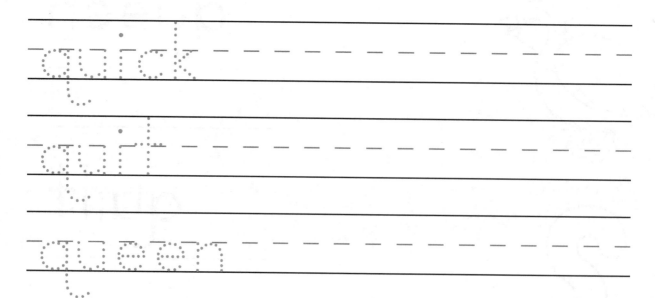

© Shell Education

Name: _____   Date: _____

Work with me to a G.

Directions: Start at each star. Connect the dots.
Then, write your own pattern.

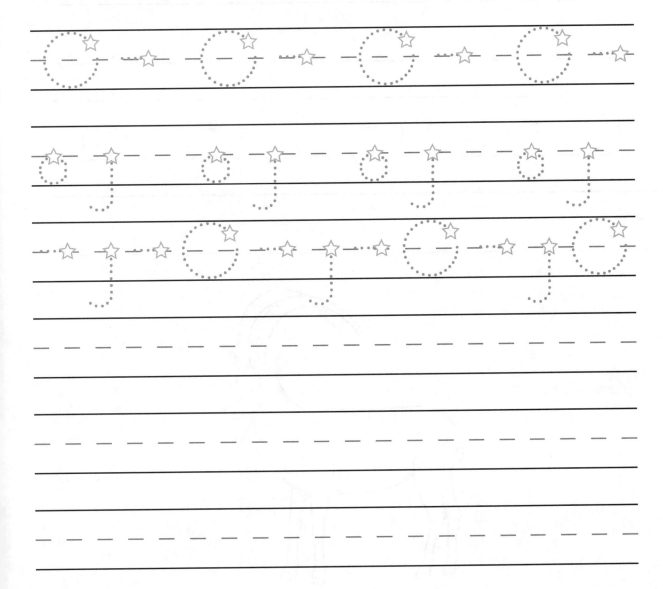

Name: _____ Date: _____

Directions: Follow the arrows. Trace each letter. Then, write your own letters to fill the lines.

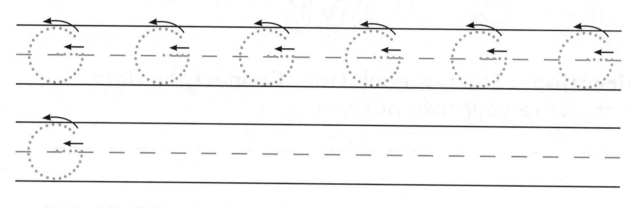

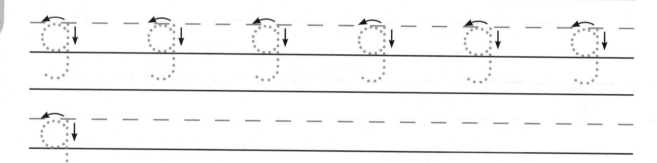

© Shell Education

Name: _____ Date: _____

Directions: Trace the letters. Then, write the missing letters to complete the words.

get   e

go   o

good   oo

Directions: Trace the letters. Then, write the missing letters to complete the sentence.

George goes golfing and is very good.

eor e oe ol ng
a d s v y oo .

Name: _____ Date: _____

Directions: Use your best handwriting to finish the sentences with things you like doing. Read the words in the box for ideas.

Activity

I am _____ .

I am _____ .

I am _____ .

running

thinking

writing

jumping

learning

practicing

sleeping

130194—180 Days of Printing: Advanced   © Shell Education

Name: _____ Date: _____

Directions: Trace each letter. Then, write your own letters to fill the lines.

G - - - - - - - - - - - - - - - -

g - - - - - - - - - - - - - - - -

Q - - - - - - - - - - - - - - - -

q - - - - - - - - - - - - - - - -

Directions: Trace each letter. Then, write the sentence again.

I go to the park.

- - - - - - - - - - - - - - - -

Review

Name: _____ Date: _____

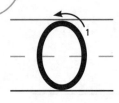

Curve all the way around like a hero, that's the way we write zero!

Directionality and Strokes

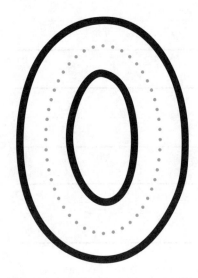

Directions: Trace each number. Then, write your own numbers to fill the lines.

1
2
3
4
5

6
7
8
9
10

Name: _____   Date: _____

O zero

Directions: Trace each number. Then, write your own numbers to fill the lines.

© Shell Education   130194—180 Days of Printing: Advanced

Name: _____ Date: _____

Directions: Trace each number to complete the math problems.

$$1 - 1 = 0$$

$$10 + 10 = 20$$

$$11 - 1 = 10$$

Directions: Solve each math problem.

$$20 + 10 = \underline{\hphantom{000}}$$

$$50 + 50 = \underline{\hphantom{000}}$$

A zebra with zero stripes!

180   130194—180 Days of Printing: Advanced   © Shell Education

Sentence Practice

Name: _____ Date: _____

Directions: Trace along the dots. Color the picture.

Name: _____ Date: _____

Review

Directions: Trace each letter and number. Then, write your own letters and numbers to fill the lines.

Directions: Trace each letter. Then, write the sentence again.

I like to run.

Name: _____ Date: _____

Lines curve around to write an *S*.

Directions: Start at each star. Connect the dots. Then, write your own letters to fill the lines.

Name: _____ Date: _____

Print Uppercase and Lowercase

Directions: Follow the arrows. Trace each letter. Then, write your own letters to fill the lines.

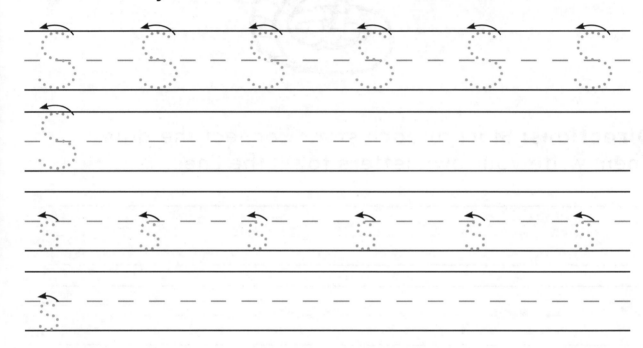

© Shell Education

Name: _____ Date: _____

Directions: Trace the letters. Then, write the missing letters to complete the words.

am   am

a   a

om   om

Directions: Trace the letters. Then, write the missing letters to complete the sentence.

Sammy ash
I e an wiche.

amm   a s h
I e an   iche.

Name: _____ Date: _____

Directions: Trace the lines. Then, color the picture.

Activity

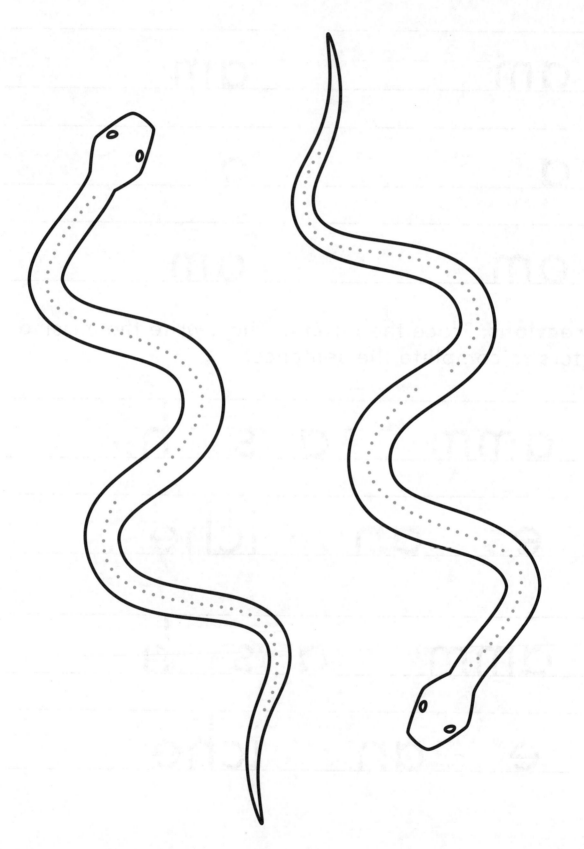

 © Shell Education

Name: _____ Date: _____

Directions: Trace each letter. Then, write your own letters to fill the lines.

R

r

S

s

Directions: Trace each letter. Then, write the sentence two more times.

I see a tree.

Review

Name: _____ Date: _____

Directionality and Strokes

Hook the line to make a J!

Directions: Start at each star. Connect the dots. Then, practice writing on your own.

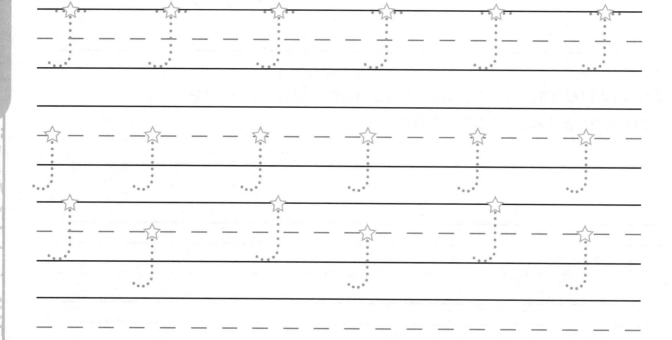

130194—180 Days of Printing: Advanced
© Shell Education

Name: _____ Date: _____

Directions: Follow the arrows. Trace each letter.
Then, write your own letters to fill the lines.

Print Uppercase and Lowercase

Name: _____ Date: _____

Directions: Trace the letters. Then, write the missing letters to complete the words and name.

Sentence Practice

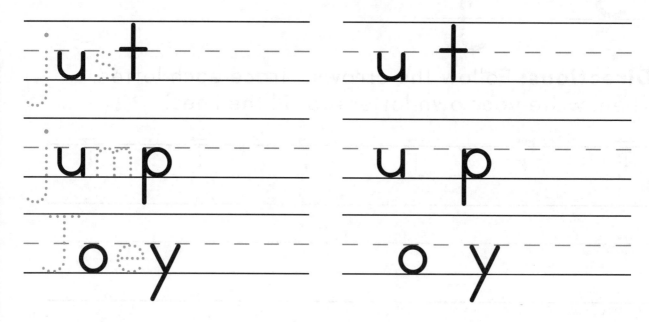

Directions: Trace the letters. Write the missing letters to complete the sentence. Then, write the sentence on your own.

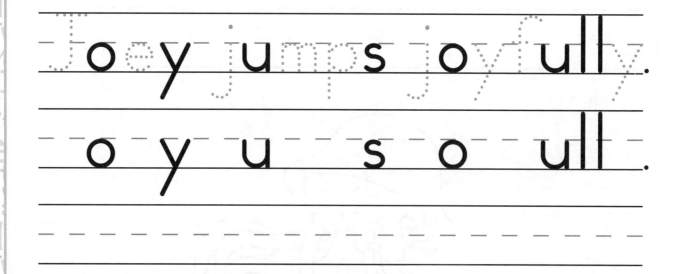

© Shell Education

Name: _____ Date: _____

Directions: Connect the dots. Then, color the picture.

Name: _____ Date: _____

Directions: Trace each word. Then, write the sentence.

I like to run.

Review

Directions: Finish each sentence.

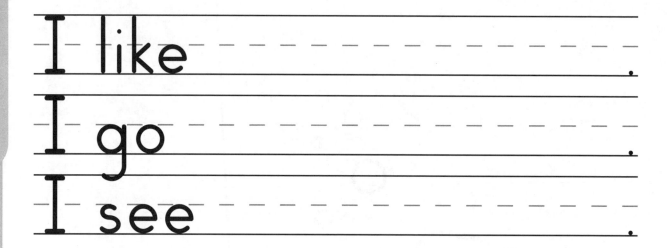

I like _____ .

I go _____ .

I see _____ .

© Shell Education

Lowercase Letter Guide

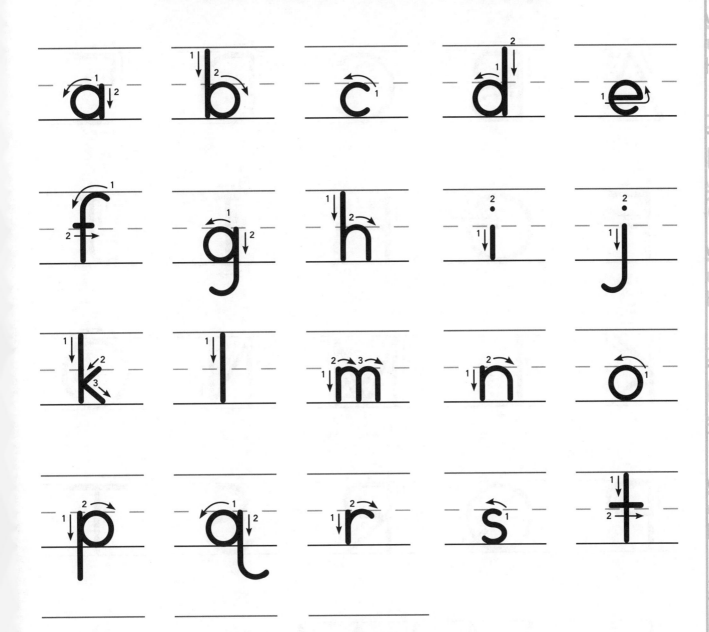

© Shell Education

Uppercase Letter Guide

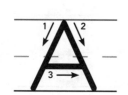

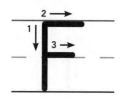

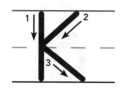 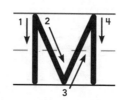 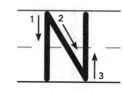 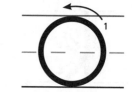

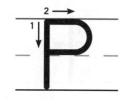  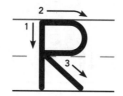  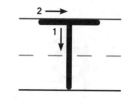

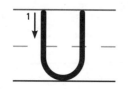 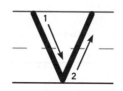 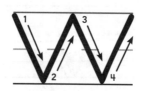

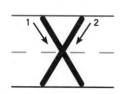 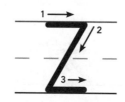

 © Shell Education

Number Guide

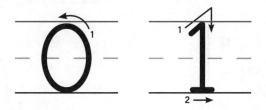

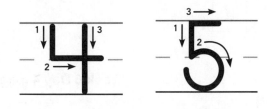

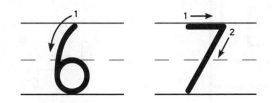

Answer Key

There are many open-ended pages and writing prompts in this book. For those activities, the answers will vary. Examples are given as needed.

Week 1 Day 4 (page 16)

N	K	h	s	K	Y	u
L	Y	N	W	H	I	x
L	X	K	a	q	I	Y
L	J	d	j	E	I	D
L	S	H	k	p	I	G
L	R	B	Y	X	I	Z
L	M	K	H	v	I	e
L	L	L	L	Y	I	N
O	Y	H	c	P	E	K

Week 5 Day 4 (page 36)

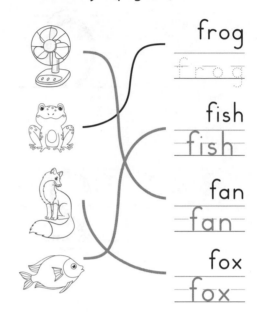

Week 2 Day 4 (page 21)

Week 6 Day 4 (page 41)

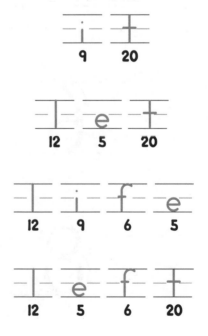

    © Shell Education

Answer Key *(cont.)*

Week 9 Day 4 (page 56)

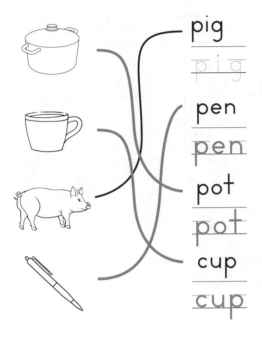

pig
pig

pen
pen

pot
pot

cup
cup

Week 13 Day 4 (page 76)

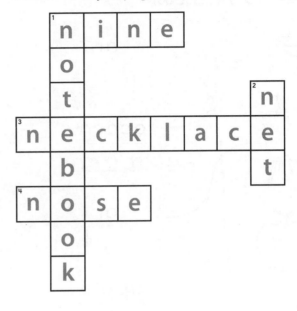

Week 11 Day 4 (page 66)

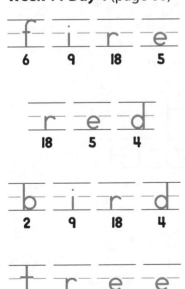

f i r e
6 9 18 5

r e d
18 5 4

b i r d
2 9 18 4

t r e e
20 18 5 5

Week 14 Day 4 (page 81)

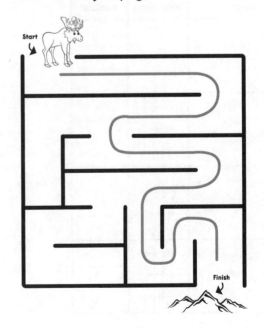

Answer Key *(cont.)*

Week 15 Day 4 (page 86)

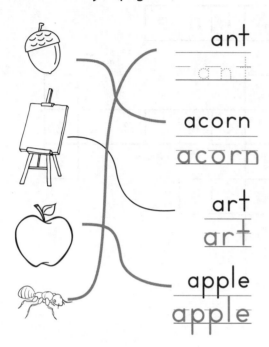

Week 16 Day 4 (page 91)

Count	Tally Mark	Number
(4 pigs)	⁞⁞⁞⁞	4
(ants)	⊞⊞ ⁞⁞	12
(8 apples)	⊞⊞ ⁞⁞⁞	8
(turtles)	⊞⊞ ⊞⊞ ⊞⊞	15

Week 18 Day 4 (page 101)

Week 20 Day 4 (page 111)

a n
1   14

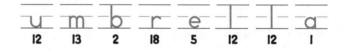

u m b r e l l a
12 13 2 18 5 12 12 1

Week 23 Day 4 (page 126)

Week 26 Day 4 (page 141)

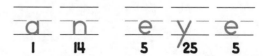

a n   e y e
1 14   5 25 5

Answer Key *(cont.)*

Week 30 Day 4 (page 161)

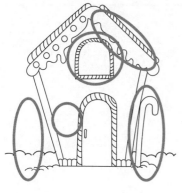

Week 32 Day 4 (page 171)

Suggested Websites

Website Title	Address	Content
ABC Mouse	www.abcmouse.com	alphabet, phonics
Learning A–Z	www.learninga-z.com	alphabet, phonics
Starfall	www.starfall.com	alphabet, phonics, emergent reading
Storybots	www.storybots.com	songs with videos for A-to-Z letters

Digital Resources

Accessing the Digital Resources

The digital resources can be downloaded by following these steps:

1. Go to **www.tcmpub.com/digital**
2. Use the ISBN number to redeem the digital resources.
3. Respond to the question using the book.
4. Follow the prompts on the Content Cloud website to sign in or create a new account.
5. The redeemed content will now be on your My Content screen. Click on the product to look through the Digital Resources. All files can be downloaded, while some files can also be previewed, opened, and shared.

   • Please note: Some files provided for download have large file sizes. Download times for these larger files vary based on your download speed.

Contents of the Digital Resources

Activities

• Hands-on practice for writing uppercase and lowercase letters
• Sentence-writing practice
• Handwriting lines for printing activities

    © Shell Education